FIFTY MAJOR DOCUMENTS
OF THE TWENTIETH CENTURY

LOUIS L. SNYDER

Professor of History
The City College of New York

AN ANVIL ORIGINAL
under the general editorship of
LOUIS L. SNYDER

D. VAN NOSTRAND COMPANY, INC.
PRINCETON, NEW JERSEY
TORONTO   LONDON
NEW YORK

To
DR. EDMUND ZIMAN

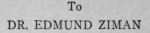

D. VAN NOSTRAND COMPANY, INC.

120 Alexander St., Princeton, New Jersey (*Principal office*) ; 24 West 40th St., New York 18, New York
D. VAN NOSTRAND COMPANY (Canada), LTD.
25 Hollinger Rd., Toronto 16, Canada
D. VAN NOSTRAND COMPANY, LTD.
358, Kensington High Street, London, W.14, England

Library of Congress Catalog Card No. 55-6236

PRINTED IN THE UNITED STATES OF AMERICA

PREFACE

It is the purpose of this volume to provide in convenient form the texts of fifty major documents in the history of the world in the last half century. It is prepared in the belief that students as well as the intelligent general reader should consult the raw materials out of which the compressed treatments of textbooks are constructed.

The items selected are those which, in the opinion of the editor, have had the most important influence on the major developments of the twentieth-century world. The student of contemporary affairs is somewhat handicapped by the fact that historians do not as yet possess the proper perspective to interpret developments that have occurred in recent years. The documents concerning important recent historical developments will give him the basis upon which he can form his own judgments.

Wherever possible the documents have been reproduced in full text, but in some cases it has been necessary to present extracts in order to reduce the length of the selection. In the latter event, an attempt has been made to keep the essential thought of the given subject. Brief introductions to each document give the historical background and state the importance of the selection.

Louis L. Snyder

TABLE OF CONTENTS

THE *DAILY TELEGRAPH* INTERVIEW, OCTOBER 28, 1908 [1]

On October 28, 1908, *The Daily Telegraph* of London published an account of an interview between Kaiser William II and an unnamed British subject—one of the most significant interviews of the century. While appearing to present himself as a lover of peace, the Kaiser, through his own words, showed himself to be an advocate of the iron-fist policy in international relations. Anxious to allay British anxiety over Germany's big navy plans by using an argument that was a characteristic blending of distorted historical fact and offensive flattery, he succeeded only in alienating both Englishmen and Germans. His *faux pas* was an incredible mistake that raised a storm of protest in both England and Germany and nearly led to the Kaiser's abdication. Historically, the *Daily Telegraph* interview marked a culminating point in Anglo-German political, economic, and naval rivalry that was to contribute to the outbreak of the catastrophe of 1914.

✸   ✸   ✸

We have received the following communication from a source of such unimpeachable authority that we can without hesitation comment on the obvious message which it conveys to the attention of the public.

Discretion is the first and last quality requisite in a diplomatist, and should still be observed by those who, like myself, have long passed from public into private life. Yet moments sometimes occur in the history of nations

[1] *London Daily Telegraph*, October 28, 1908.

when a calculated indiscretion proves of the highest public service, and it is for that reason that I have decided to make known the substance of a lengthy conversation which it is my privilege to have had with His Majesty the German Emperor. I do so in the hope that it may help to remove that obstinate misconception of the character of the Kaiser's feelings toward England which, I fear, is deeply rooted in the Englishman's breast. It is the Emperor's sincere wish that it should be eradicated. He has given repeated proofs of his desire by word and deed. But, to speak frankly, his patience is sorely tried, now that he finds himself so continually misrepresented, and has so often experienced the mortification of finding that any momentary improvement of relations is followed by renewed outbursts of prejudice and a prompt return to the old attitude of suspicion.

As I have said, His Majesty honored me with a long conversation, and spoke with impulsive and unusual frankness.

"You English," he said, "are mad, mad, mad as March hares. What has come over you that you are so completely given over to suspicions quite unworthy of a great nation? What more can I do than I have done? I declared with all the emphasis at my command, in my speech at Guildhall, that my heart is set upon peace, and that it is one of my dearest wishes to live on the best of terms with England. Have I ever been false to my word? Falsehood and prevarication are alien to my nature. My actions ought to speak for themselves, but you listen not to them but to those who misinterpret and distort them. That is a personal insult which I feel and resent. To be forever misjudged, to have my repeated offers of friendship weighed and scrutinized with jealous, mistrustful eyes, taxes my patience severely. I have said time after time that I am a friend of England, and your press —or, at least, a considerable section of it—bids the people of England refuse my proffered hand and insinuates that the other holds a dagger. How can I convince a nation against its will?

"I repeat," continued His Majesty, "that I am a friend of England, but you make things difficult for me. My task is not of the easiest. The prevailing sentiment among

large sections of the middle and lower classes of my own
people is not friendly to England. I am, therefore, so to
speak, in a minority in my own land, but it is a minority
of the best elements as it is in England with respect to
Germany. That is another reason why I resent your
refusal to accept my pledged word that I am the friend
of England. I strive without ceasing to improve relations,
and you retort that I am your archenemy. You make it
hard for me. Why is it?"

Thereupon I ventured to remind His Majesty that not
England alone, but the whole of Europe had viewed with
disapproval the recent action of Germany in allowing the
German consul to return from Tangier to Fez, and in
anticipating the joint action of France and Spain by suggesting to the Powers that the time had come to Europe
to recognize Mulai Hafiz as the new Sultan of Morocco.

His Majesty made a gesture of impatience.

"Yes," he said, "that is an excellent example of the
way in which German action is misrepresented. First,
then, as regards to the journey of Dr. Vassel. The German government, in sending Dr. Vassel back to his post
at Fez, was only guided by the wish that he should look
after the private interests of German subjects in that city,
who cried for help and protection after the long absence
of a consular representative. And why not send him? Are
those who charge Germany with having stolen a march
on other Powers aware that the French consular representative had already been in Fez for several months before Dr. Vassel set out? Then, as to the recognition of
Mulai Hafiz. The press of Europe has complained with
much acerbity that Germany ought not to have suggested
his recognition until he had notified to Europe his full
acceptance of the Act of Algeciras, as being binding upon
him as Sultan of Morocco and successor of his brother.
My answer is that Mulai Hafiz notified the Powers to
that effect weeks ago, before the decisive battle was
fought. He sent, as far back as the middle of last July,
an intentional communication to the governments of Germany, France, and Great Britain, containing an explicit
acknowledgment that he was prepared to recognize all
the obligations toward Europe which were incurred by
Abdal-Aziz during his sultanate. The German government

interpreted that communication as a final and authoritative expression of Mulai Hafiz's intentions, and therefore they considered that there was no reason to wait until he had sent a second communication before recognizing him as the *de facto* Sultan of Morocco, who had succeeded to his brother's throne by right of victory in the field."

I suggested to His Majesty that an important and influential section of the German press had placed a very different interpretation upon the action of the German government, and, in fact, had given it their effusive approbation because they saw in it a strong act instead of mere words, and a decisive indication that Germany was once more about to intervene in the shaping of events in Morocco.

"There are mischief-makers," replied the Emperor, "in both countries. I will not attempt to weigh their relative capacity for misrepresentation. But the facts are as I have stated. There has been nothing in Germany's recent action with regard to Morocco which runs contrary to the explicit declaration of my love for peace which I made both at Guildhall and in my latest speech at Strasbourg."

His Majesty then reverted to the subject uppermost in his mind—his proved friendship for England. "I have referred," he said, "to the speeches in which I have done all that a sovereign can do to proclaim my good will. But, as actions speak louder than words, let me also refer to my acts. It is commonly believed in England that throughout the South African War Germany was hostile to her. German opinion undoubtedly was hostile—bitterly hostile. But what of official Germany? Let my critics ask themselves what brought to a sudden stop, and, indeed, to absolute collapse, the European tour of the Boer delegates, who were striving to obtain European intervention? They were feted in Holland, France gave them a rapturous welcome. They wished to come to Berlin, where the German people would have crowned them with flowers. But when they asked me to receive them—I refused. The agitation immediately died away, and the delegation returned empty-handed. Was that, I ask, the action of a secret enemy?

"Again, when the struggle was at its height, the Ger-

man government was invited by the governments of
France and Russia to join with them in calling upon
England to put an end to the war. The moment had come,
they said, not only to save the Boer Republics, but also
to humiliate England to the dust. What was my reply?
I said that so far from Germany joining in any concerted European action to put pressure upon England and
bring about her downfall, Germany would always keep
aloof from politics that could bring her into complica-
tions with a sea power like England. Posterity will one
day read the exact terms of the telegram—now in the
archives of Windsor Castle—in which I informed the
sovereign of England of the answer I had returned to
the Powers which then sought to compass her fall. Englishmen who now insult me by doubting my word should
know what were my actions in the hour of their ad-
versity.

"Nor was that all. Just at the time of your Black
Week, in the December of 1899, when disasters followed
one another in rapid succession, I received a letter from
Queen Victoria, my revered grandmother, written in sorrow and affliction, and bearing manifest traces of the
anxieties which were preying upon her mind and health.
I at once returned a sympathetic reply. Nay, I did more.
I bade one of my officers procure for me as exact an
account as he could obtain of the number of combatants
in South Africa on both sides and of the actual position
of the opposing forces. With the figures before me, I
worked out what I considered the best plan of campaign
under the circumstances, and submitted it to my General
Staff for their criticism. Then, I dispatched it to England, and that document, likewise, is among the state
papers at Windsor Castle, awaiting the severely impartial verdict of history. And, as a matter of curious coin-
cidence, let me add that the plan which I formulated ran
very much on the same lines as that which was actually
adopted by Lord Roberts, and carried by him into successful operation. Was that, I repeat, an act of one who
wished England ill? Let Englishmen be just and say!

"But, you will say, what of the German navy? Surely,
that is a menace to England! Against whom but England
are my squadrons being prepared? If England is not in

the minds of those Germans who are bent on creating a powerful fleet, why is Germany asked to consent to such new and heavy burdens of taxation? My answer is clear. Germany is a young and growing empire. She has a worldwide commerce which is rapidly expanding, and to which the legitimate ambition of patriotic Germans refuses to assign any bounds. Germany must have a powerful fleet to protect that commerce and her manifold interests in even the most distant seas. She expects those interests to go on growing, and she must be able to champion them manfully in any quarter of the globe. Her horizons stretch far away. She must be prepared for any eventualities in the Far East. Who can foresee what may take place in the Pacific in the days to come, days not so distant as some believe, but days, at any rate, for which all European Powers with Far Eastern interests ought steadily to prepare? Look at the accomplished rise of Japan; think of the possible national awakening of China; and then judge of the vast problems of the Pacific. Only those Powers which have great navies will be listened to with respect when the future of the Pacific comes to be solved; and if for that reason only Germany must have a powerful fleet. It may even be that England herself will be glad that Germany has a fleet when they speak together on the same side in the great debates of the future."

Such was the purport of the Emperor's conversation. He spoke with all the earnestness which marks his manner when speaking on deeply pondered subjects. I would ask my fellow countrymen who value the cause of peace to weigh what I have written, and to revise, if necessary, their estimate of the Kaiser and his friendship for England by His Majesty's own words. If they had enjoyed the privilege, which was mine, of hearing them spoken, they would doubt no longer either His Majesty's firm desire to live on the best of terms with England or his growing impatience at the persistent mistrust with which his offer of friendship is too often received.

— 2 —

THE AUSTRO-HUNGARIAN ULTIMATUM TO SERBIA, JULY 23, 1914 [2]

On June 28, 1914, Archduke Francis Ferdinand, the heir-presumptive to the throne of Austria-Hungary, and his wife were assassinated at Sarajevo, the capital of Bosnia, by a fanatically patriotic Bosnian youth. While the Serbian government was not responsible for the deed, it probably had some knowledge of the plot, but took no steps to prevent its execution. The assassination, generally condemned as an abominable crime, at first was regarded as merely another incident in the interminable Balkan quarrels, but this was the spark that began a world-wide conflagration.

Eager to eliminate Serbia as an obstacle in the Balkans, Austria-Hungary seized the opportunity provided by the assassination to settle accounts with the obstreperous Slavs. Being assured of German support, the Austro-Hungarian Foreign Minister, Count von Berchtold, sent a forty-eight hour ultimatum to Serbia demanding the suppression of anti-Austrian propaganda, the dissolution of the *Union or Death* society, and permission for Austrian officials to assist in suppressing disorders in Serbia. Serbia, supported by Russia, replied on July 25 that she would submit the issue to the Hague Tribunal, but refused to permit Austrian officials to function on Serbian soil, deeming such a concession a surrender of Serbian sovereignty. The war began when Austria-Hungary denounced Serbia's conciliatory reply as unsatisfactory.

[2] Max Montgelas and Walter Schückling, eds., *Outbreak of the World War: Documents Collected by Karl Kautsky* (Carnegie Endowment for International Peace, New York, 1924), Supplement I, 603-06.

The Austria-Hungarian Minister for Foreign Affairs, Berchtold, to the Minister at Belgrade, von Giesl

Vienna, July 22, 1914

Your Excellency will present the following note to the Royal Government on the afternoon of Thursday, July 23:

On the 31st of March, 1909, the Royal Serbian Minister at the Court of Vienna made, in the name of his Government, the following declaration to the Imperial and Royal Government:

> Serbia recognizes that her rights were not affected by the state of affairs created in Bosnia, and states that she will accordingly accommodate herself to the decisions to be reached by the Powers in connection with Article 25 of the Treaty of Berlin. Serbia, in accepting the advice of the Great Powers, binds herself to desist from the attitude of protest and opposition which she has assumed with regard to the annexation since October last, and she furthermore binds herself to alter the tendency of her present policy toward Austria-Hungary, and to live on the footing of friendly and neighborly relations with the latter in the future.

Now the history of the past few years, and particularly the painful events of the 28th of June, have proved the existence of a subversive movement in Serbia, whose object it is to separate certain portions of its territory from the Austro-Hungarian Monarchy. This movement, which came into being under the very eyes of the Serbian Government, subsequently found expression outside of the territory of the Kingdom in acts of terrorism, in a number of attempts at assassination, and in murders.

Far from fulfilling the formal obligations contained in its declaration of the 31st of March, 1909, the Royal Serbian Government has done nothing to suppress this movement. It has tolerated the criminal activities of the various unions and associations directed against the Monarchy, the unchecked utterances of the press, the glorification of the authors of assassinations, the participation of officers and officials in subversive intrigues; it has tolerated an unhealthy propaganda in its public instruction; and it has tolerated, finally, every manifestation which could betray the people of Serbia into hatred of the Monarchy and contempt for its institutions.

This toleration of which the Royal Serbian Government was guilty, was still in evidence at that moment when the events of the twenty-eighth of June exhibited to the whole world the dreadful consequences of such tolerance.

It is clear from the statements and confessions of the criminal authors of the assassination of the twenty-eighth of June, that the murder at Sarajevo was conceived at Belgrade, that the murderers received the weapons and the bombs with which they were equipped from Serbian officers and officials who belonged to the *Narodna Odbrana,* and, finally, that the dispatch of the criminals and of their weapons to Bosnia was arranged and effected under the conduct of Serbian frontier authorities.

The results brought out by the inquiry no longer permit the Imperial and Royal Government to maintain the attitude of patient tolerance which it has observed for years toward those agitations which center at Belgrade and are spread thence into the territories of the Monarchy. Instead, these results impose upon the Imperial and Royal Government the obligation to put an end to those intrigues, which constitute a standing menace to the peace of the Monarchy.

In order to attain this end, the Imperial and Royal Government finds itself compelled to demand that the Serbian Government give official assurance that it will condemn the propaganda directed against Austria-Hungary, that is to say, the whole body of the efforts whose ultimate object it is to separate from the Monarchy territories that belong to it; and that it will obligate itself to suppress with all the means at its command this criminal and terroristic propaganda.

In order to give these assurances a character of solemnity, the Royal Serbian Government will publish on the first page of its official organ of July 26/13, the following declaration:

"The Royal Serbian Government condemns the propaganda directed against Austria-Hungary, that is to say, the whole body of the efforts whose ultimate object it is to separate from the Austro-Hungarian Monarchy territories that belong to it, and it most sincerely regrets the dreadful consequences of these criminal transactions.

"The Royal Serbian Government regrets that Serbian officers and officials should have taken part in the above-mentioned propaganda and thus have endangered the friendly and neighborly relations, to the cultivation of which the Royal Government had most solemnly pledged itself by its declarations of March 31, 1909.

"The Royal Government, which disapproves and repels every idea and every attempt to interfere in the destinies of the population of whatever portion of Austria-Hungary, regards it as its duty most expressly to call attention of the officers, officials and the whole population of the kingdom to the fact that for the future it will proceed with the utmost rigor against any persons who shall become guilty of any such activities, activities to prevent and to suppress which, the Government will bend every effort."

This declaration shall be brought to the attention of the Royal army simultaneously by an order of the day from His Majesty the King, and by publication in the official organ of the army.

The Royal Serbian Government will furthermore pledge itself:

1. to suppress every publication which shall incite to hatred and contempt of the Monarchy, and the general tendency of which shall be directed against the territorial integrity of the latter;

2. to proceed at once to the dissolution of the *Narodna Odbrana,* to confiscate all of its means of propaganda, and in the same manner to proceed against the other unions and associations in Serbia which occupy themselves with propaganda against Austria-Hungary; the Royal Government will take such measures as are necessary to make sure that the dissolved associations may not continue their activities under other names or in other forms;

3. to eliminate without delay from public instruction in Serbia, everything, whether connected with the teaching corps or with the methods of teaching, that serves or

may serve to nourish the propaganda against Austria-Hungary;

4. to remove from the military and administrative service in general all officers and officials who have been guilty of carrying on the propaganda against Austria-Hungary, whose names the Imperial and Royal Government reserves the right to make known to the Royal Government when communicating the material evidence now in its possession;

5. to agree to the coöperation in Serbia of the organs of the Imperial and Royal Government in the suppression of the subversive movement directed against the integrity of the Monarchy;

6. to institute a judicial inquiry against every participant in the conspiracy of the twenty-eighth of June who may be found in Serbian territory; the organs of the Imperial and Royal Government delegated for this purpose will take part in the proceedings held for this purpose;

7. to undertake with all haste the arrest of Major Voislav Tankositch and of one Milan Ciganovitch, a Serbian official, who have been compromised by the results of the inquiry;

8. by efficient measures to prevent the participation of Serbian authorities in the smuggling of weapons and explosives across the frontier; to dismiss from the service and to punish severely those members of the Frontier Service at Schabats and Losnitza who assisted the authors of the crime of Sarajevo to cross the frontier;

9. to make explanations to the Imperial and Royal Government concerning the unjustifiable utterances of high Serbian functionaries in Serbia and abroad, who, without regard for their official position, have not hesitated to express themselves in a manner hostile toward Austria-Hungary since the assassination of the twenty-eighth of June;

10. to inform the Imperial and Royal Government without delay of the execution of the measures comprised in the foregoing points.

The Imperial and Royal Government awaits the reply of the Royal Government by Saturday, the twenty-fifth instant, at 6 p.m., at the latest.

EXTRACTS FROM BETHMANN-HOLLWEG'S SPEECH TO THE REICHSTAG, AUGUST 4, 1914[3]

The German case in 1914 was based on the claims that Germany had been denied her proper share of colonies in an age of imperialism, that she needed more *Lebensraum* (living space), and that the Great Powers had tried to throttle Germany by their *Einkreisungspolitik* (encirclement policy). The German Chancellor, von Bethmann-Hollweg, stated the German point of view in this address to the German Reichstag shortly after outbreak of the war.

✦ ✦ ✦

A tremendous fate has fallen upon Europe. While we have sought to maintain the prestige of the German Empire in the eyes of the world, we have lived for forty-four years in peace and we have protected the peace of Europe. In this work for peace we have become strong and mighty, therefore we are envied. We have suffered with a long-enduring patience, while in the East and West, under the excuse that Germany lusts for war, hatred for us has been nurtured and chains have been cast to bind us. The wind which blows from those directions have now become a storm.

We desired only to live in peaceful work, content with a silent oath that has echoed from the Emperor down to the youngest recruit. Our sword shall only emerge from its sheath to defend a just cause. [*Loud applause.*] The day on which we must draw it has dawned against our will and against our honest endeavors. Russia has applied a burning torch against the house of peace. [*Loud cries of*

---

[3] As reported in the *Berliner Tageblatt,* August 5, 1914.

"True! True!"] Today we stand in a war with Russia and France that has been forced upon us. . . .

The Emperor has ordered that the French frontier should be respected. This order has been strictly obeyed, with one single exception. France, which mobilized at the same time as we did, declared that she would respect a ten-kilometre zone along her frontiers. [*Cries of indignation.*] And what actually happened? Their aviators have thrown bombs, their cavalry patrols have violated our territory, and troops have broken into Alsace-Lorraine. [*Indignation.*] Thereupon, France, even though war had not yet been declared, attacked our territories. . . .

We stand now in a defensive position, and necessity knows no law! [*Shouts of "True! True!"*] Our troops have occupied Luxembourg, perhaps they have already entered Belgium. [*Loud applause.*] That is a breach of international law. It is true that the French Government declared in Brussels that it would respect Belgian neutrality as long as their enemy respected it. But we were aware that France was ready to invade Belgium. [*Cries of indignation.*]

France could wait. We could not. A French attack on our flank on the Lower Rhine might have had disastrous consequences for us. Thus, we had to ignore the protests of the Luxembourg and Belgian Governments.

The injustice which we have thereby committed, we shall try to make good as soon as our military goal is attained. Anyone who fights for the highest purpose, as we are doing, can only think of how he can win his way through. [*Waves of applause.*]. . . .

Gentlemen, we stand shoulder to shoulder with Austria-Hungary.

In the matter of England's attitude, the statement made yesterday in the House of Commons by Sir Edward Grey has made the position of the English Government very clear.

We have informed the English Government that, as long as England remains neutral, our fleet will not attack the north coast of France. Furthermore, we shall not violate the territorial integrity and independence of Belgium. I repeat this declaration before the whole world. . . .

Gentlemen, so much for what has happened up to now!

I repeat the words of the Emperor: 'We enter the struggle with a clear conscience!' [*Great enthusiasm.*] We fight for the fruits of our labors in peace, for the heritage of our great past, and for our future. The fifty years have not yet passed in which Moltke said we should be vigilant with our arms to defend the heritage and achievements of 1870. The hour of great trial has tolled for our people. We look forward to it with complete confidence. [*Tremendous applause.*]

Our army is now in the field, our fleet is prepared, and behind them stands the German nation [*waves of enthusiastic applause and hand-clapping in the whole Reichstag*] —the entire German nation! [*These words were accompanied by a gesture toward the Social Democrats. New outbursts of applause, in which the Social Democrats also joined.*]

Gentlemen, you know your duty in its entirety. The vote for war credits needs no further arguments. I beseech you to pass it quickly. [*Loud applause.*]

— 4 —

THE ZIMMERMANN NOTE, JANUARY 19, 1917[4]

On January 19, 1917, the German Foreign Secretary, Alfred Zimmermann, sent a note to the German Ambassador in Mexico proposing to Mexico an alliance providing for a joint war against the United States. Intercep-

[4] *Congressional Record,* LVI (March 1, 1917), Part 1, pp. 680-81.

tion and publication of the note in the United States greatly strengthened the demand for war, especially in the hitherto lukewarm Southwest, which Germany proposed to cede to Mexico.

✓   ✓   ✓

Berlin, January 19, 1917

On the first of February we intend to begin submarine warfare unrestricted. In spite of this, it is our intention to endeavor to keep neutral the United States of America.

If this attempt is not successful, we propose an alliance on the following basis with Mexico: That we shall make war together and together make peace. We shall give general financial support, and it is understood that Mexico is to reconquer the lost territory in New Mexico, Texas, and Arizona. The details are left to you for settlement.

You are instructed to inform the President of Mexico of the above in the greatest confidence as soon as it is certain that there will be an outbreak of war with the United States and suggest that the President of Mexico, on his own initiative, should communicate with Japan suggesting adherence at once to this plan; at the same time, offer to mediate between Germany and Japan.

Please call to the attention of the President of Mexico that the employment of ruthless submarine warfare now promises to compel England to make peace in a few months.

ZIMMERMANN

PRESIDENT WILSON'S WAR MESSAGE, APRIL 2, 1917[5]

Public opinion in the United States was hesitant and confused at the outbreak of World War I in 1914. President Wilson at once declared American neutrality and came forward as a champion of neutral rights. The United States protested vigorously against British interference with neutral trade, but there was even more resentment against Germany's submarine campaign. The sinking of the *Lusitania* on May 7, 1915 aroused intense feelings when it became known that many Americans were among the 1,198 men, women, and children who perished. Germany modified her submarine campaign in response to repeated American notes of protest. On January 9, 1917, the German Imperial War Council decided to resume a policy of unrestricted submarine warfare. After three American ships were sent to the bottom on March 18, Congress was called in extra session on April 2. In an eloquent speech, from which extracts are printed below, the American President declared that the course of the German government was nothing less than a state of war, and he urged Congress to accept the challenge. A joint resolution declaring that a state of war existed passed the Senate on April 4 with five votes against it, and the House on April 6 with fifty votes in the negative.

Gentlemen of the Congress:

I have called the Congress into extraordinary session because there are serious, very serious, choices of policy to be made, and made immmediately, which it was neither right nor constitutionally permissible that I should assume the responsibility of making.

[5] Woodrow Wilson, *War Message* (65th Congress, 1st session, Senate Document No. 5 (Washington, 1917), pp. 3-8.

On the third of February last I officially laid before you the extraordinary announcement of the Imperial German Government that on and after the first day of February it was its purpose to put aside all restraints of law and humanity and use its submarines to sink every vessel that sought to approach either the ports of Great Britain and Ireland or the western coasts of Europe or any of the ports controlled by the enemies of Germany within the Mediterranean. That had seemed to be the object of the German submarine warfare earlier in the war, but since April of last year the Imperial Government had somewhat restrained the commanders of its undersea craft. . . . The new policy has swept every restriction aside. . . .

I was for a little while unable to believe that such things would in fact be done by any government that had hitherto subscribed to the humane practices of civilized nations. . . .

It is a war against all nations. American ships have been sunk, American lives taken, in ways which it has stirred us very deeply to learn of, but the ships and people of other neutral and friendly nations have been sunk and overwhelmed in the waters in the same way. There has been no discrimination. The challenge is to all mankind. Each nation must decide for itself how it will meet it. The choice we make for ourselves must be made with a moderation of counsel and a temperateness of judgment befitting our character and our motives as a nation. We must put excited feeling away. Our motive will not be revenge or the victorious assertion of the physical might of the nation, but only the vindication of right, of human right, of which we are only a single champion. . . .

With a profound sense of the solemn and even tragical character of the step I am taking and of the grave responsibilities which it involves, but in unhesitating obedience to what I deem my constitutional duty, I advise that the Congress declare the recent course of the Imperial German Government to be in fact nothing less than war against the government and people of the United States; that it formally accept the status of belligerent which has thus been thrust upon it; and that it take immediate steps not only to put the country into a more thorough state of defense but also to exert all its power and employ all its resources to bring the Government of the German Empire to terms and end the war. . . .

We have no quarrel with the German people. We have no feeling towards them but one of sympathy and friendship. It was not upon their impulse that their government acted in entering this war. It was not with their previous knowledge or approval. It was a war determined upon as wars used to be determined upon in the old unhappy days when peoples were nowhere consulted by their rulers and wars were provoked and waged in the interest of dynasties or of little groups of ambitious men who were accustomed to use their fellow men as pawns and tools. Self-governed nations do not fill their neighbor states with spies or set the course of intrigue to bring about some critical posture of affairs which will give them an opportunity to strike and make conquest. Such designs can be successfully worked out only under cover and where no one has the right to ask questions. Cunningly contrived plans of deception or aggression, carried, it may be, from generation to generation, can be worked out and kept from the light only within the privacy of courts or behind the carefully guarded confidences of a narrow and privileged class. They are happily impossible where public opinion commands and insists upon full information concerning all the nation's affairs. . . .

It is a distressing and oppressive duty, Gentlemen of the Congress, which I have performed in thus addressing you. There are, it may be, many months of fiery trial and sacrifice ahead of us. It is a fearful thing to lead this great peaceful people into war, into the most terrible and disastrous of all wars, civilization itself seeming to be in the balance. But the right is more precious than peace, and we shall fight for the things which we have always carried nearest to our hearts—for democracy, for the right of those who submit to authority to have a voice in their own governments, for the rights and liberties of small nations, for a universal dominion of right by such a concert of free peoples as shall bring peace and safety to all nations and make the world itself at last free. To such a task we can dedicate our lives and our fortunes, everything that we are and everything that we have,

with the pride of those who know that the day has come
when America is privileged to spend her blood and her
might for the principles that gave her birth and happiness
and the peace which she has treasured. God helping her,
she can do no other.

— 6 —

THE BALFOUR DECLARATION ON PALESTINE, NOVEMBER 2, 1917[6]

Great Britain promised by the Balfour Declaration of
1917 to establish in Palestine "a national homeland for
the Jewish people."

✓   ✓   ✓

Foreign Office
November 2nd, 1917

Dear Lord Rothschild,

I have much pleasure in conveying to you, on behalf
of His Majesty's Government, the following declaration
of sympathy with Jewish Zionist aspirations which has
been submitted to, and approved by, the Cabinet.

His Majesty's Government view with favour the
establishment in Palestine of a National Home for
the Jewish people, and will use their best endeavours
to facilitate the achievement of this object, it being
clearly understood that nothing shall be done which
may prejudice the civil and religious rights of existing

[6] Text in L. Stein, *Zionism* (London, 1925).

non-Jewish communities in Palestine, or the rights and political status enjoyed by Jews in any other country.

I should be grateful if you would bring this declaration to the knowledge of the Zionist Federation.

Yours sincerely,

ARTHUR JAMES BALFOUR

— 7 —

THE FOURTEEN POINTS, JANUARY 8, 1918[7]

The best-known statement of war aims in World War I came from President Wilson on January 8, 1918, when he put into definite form the conditions of peace that had been left vague by other Allied statesmen. The Fourteen Points, delivered at a joint session of the two houses of Congress, and accepted only reluctantly by the Allies, made a tremendous impression in war-weary Germany. The Germans later denounced the statement as a trick deliberately designed to destroy their morale.

✔   ✔   ✔

1. Open covenants of peace, openly arrived at, after which there shall be no private international understandings of any kind but diplomacy shall proceed always frankly and in the public view.

2. Absolute freedom of navigation upon the seas, out-

[7] United States Serial 7443. Document No. 765, January 8, 1918.

side territorial waters, alike in peace and in war, except as the seas may be closed in whole or in part by international action for the enforcement of international covenants.

3. The removal, so far as possible, of all economic barriers and the establishment of an equality of trade conditions among all the nations consenting to the peace and associating themselves for its maintenance.

4. Adequate guarantees given and taken that national armaments will be reduced to the lowest point consistent with domestic safety.

5. A free, open-minded, and absolutely impartial adjustment of all colonial claims, based upon a strict observance of the principle that in determining all such questions of sovereignty the interests of the populations concerned must have equal weight with the equitable claims of the government whose title is to be determined.

6. The evacuation of all Russian territory and such a settlement of all questions affecting Russia as will secure the best and freest coöperation of the other nations of the world in obtaining for her an unhampered and unembarrassed opportunity for the independent termination of her own political development and national policy and assure her of a sincere welcome into the society of free nations under institutions of her own choosing; and, more than a welcome, assistance also of every kind that she may need and may herself desire. The treatment accorded Russia by her sister nations in the months to come will be the acid test of their good will, of their comprehension of her needs as distinguished from their own interests, and of their intelligent and unselfish sympathy.

7. Belgium, the whole world will agree, must be evacuated and restored, without any attempt to limit the sovereignty which she enjoys in common with all other free nations. No other single act will serve as this will serve to restore confidence among the nations in the laws which they have themselves set and determined for the government of their relations with one another. Without this healing act the whole structure and validity of international law is forever impaired.

8. All French territory should be freed and the invaded portions restored, and the wrong done to France by Prus-

sia in 1871 in the matter of Alsace-Lorraine, which has unsettled the peace of the world for nearly fifty years, should be righted, in order that peace may once more be made secure in the interest of all.

9. A readjustment of the frontiers of Italy should be effected along clearly recognizable lines of nationality.

10. The peoples of Austria-Hungary, whose place among the nations we wish to see safeguarded and assured, should be accorded the freest opportunity of autonomous development.

11. Rumania, Serbia, and Montenegro should be evacuated; occupied territories restored; Serbia accorded free and secure access to the sea; and the relations of the several Balkan states to one another determined by friendly counsel along historically established lines of allegiance and nationality; and international guarantees of the political and economic independence and territorial integrity of the several Balkan states should be entered into.

12. The Turkish portions of the present Ottoman Empire should be assured a secure sovereignty, but the other nationalities which are now under Turkish rule should be assured an undoubted security of life and an absolutely unmolested opportunity of autonomous development, and the Dardanelles should be permanently opened as a free passage to the ships and commerce of all nations under international guarantees.

13. An independent Polish state should be erected which should include the territories inhabited by indisputably Polish populations, which should be assured a free and secure access to the sea, and whose political and economic independence and territorial integrity should be guaranteed by international covenant.

14. A general association of nations must be formed under specific covenants for the purpose of affording mutual guarantees of political independence and territorial integrity to great and small states alike.

THE ARMISTICE DEMANDS, NOVEMBER 10, 1918 [8]

The following terms were set by the victorious Allied powers for the armistice after World War I.

✓   ✓   ✓

1. Effective six hours after signing.
2. Immediate clearing of Belgium, France, Alsace-Lorraine, to be concluded within 14 days. Any troops remaining in these areas to be interned or taken as prisoners of war.
3. Surrender 5000 cannon (chiefly heavy), 30,000 machine guns, 3000 trench mortars, 2000 planes.
4. Evacuation of the left bank of the Rhine, Mayence, Coblence, Cologne, occupied by the enemy to a radius of 30 kilometers deep.
5. On the right bank of the Rhine a neutral zone from 30 to 40 kilometers deep, evacuation within 11 days.
6. Nothing to be removed from the territory on the left bank of the Rhine, all factories, railroads, etc. to be left intact.
7. Surrender of 5000 locomotives, 150,000 railway coaches, 10,000 trucks.
8. Maintenance of enemy occupation troops through Germany.
9. In the East all troops to withdraw behind the boundaries of August 1, 1914, fixed time not given.
10. Renunciation of the Treaties of Brest-Litovsk and Bucharest.
11. Unconditional surrender of East Africa.
12. Return of the property of the Belgian Bank, Russian and Rumanian gold.

[8] Official release by the German Government, published in the *Kreuz-Zeitung*, November 11, 1918.

13. Return of prisoners of war without reciprocity.

14. Surrender of 160 U-boats, 8 light cruisers, 6 Dreadnoughts; the rest of the fleet to be disarmed and controlled by the Allies in neutral or Allied harbors.

15. Assurance of free trade through the Cattegat Sound; clearance of mine-fields and occupation of all forts and batteries, through which transit could be hindered.

16. The blockade remains in effect. All German ships to be captured.

17. All limitations by Germany on neutral shipping to be removed.

18. Armistice lasts 30 days.

— 9 —

THE COVENANT OF THE LEAGUE OF NATIONS, 1919[9]

In the fourteenth of his famous points President Wilson suggested the formation of a general association of nations as an instrument of international coöperation. The Covenant of the League of Nations, reproduced here in full, consisted of twenty-six articles, which comprised the first twenty-six articles of each of the peace treaties following World War I. Amendments to the original draft are shown in italics. Attention is directed especially to Article 10 (agreeing to respect and preserve against external aggression the territorial integrity and existing independence of all members of the League); and Article 16

[9] From *The Assembly of the League of Nations,* Bulletin No. 6, September, 1930, League of Nations Association, Geneva.

(providing for the application of economic sanctions against any nation resorting to armed hostilities). It should also be noted that the non-permanent members of the Council were increased from four to six (September 22, 1922), to nine (September 8, 1926), to ten (October 5, 1933), and to eleven (October 10, 1936).

✓   ✓   ✓

THE HIGH CONTRACTING PARTIES,

In order to promote international coöperation and to achieve international peace and security

by the acceptance of obligations not to resort to war,

by the prescription of open, just and honorable relations between nations

by the firm establishment of the understandings of international law as the actual rule of conduct among Governments,

and by the maintenance of justice and a scrupulous respect for all treaty obligations in the dealings of organised peoples with one another,

Agree to this Covenant of the League of Nations.

ARTICLE 1. 1. The original Members of the League of Nations shall be those of the Signatories which are named in the Annex to this Covenant and also such of those other States named in the Annex as shall accede without reservation to this Covenant. Such accession shall be effected by a Declaration deposited with the Secretariat within two months of the coming into force of the Covenant. Notice thereof shall be sent to all other Members of the League.

2. Any fully self-governing State, Dominion or Colony not named in the Annex may become a Member of the League if its admission is agreed to by two-thirds of the Assembly, provided that it shall give effective guarantees of its sincere intention to observe its international obligations, and shall accept such regulations as may be prescribed by the League in regard to its military, naval and air forces and armaments.

3. Any Member of the League may, after two years' notice of its intention so to do, withdraw from the League, provided that all its international obligations and

all its obligations under this Covenant shall have been fulfilled at the time of its withdrawal.

ARTICLE 2. The action of the League under this Covenant shall be effected through the instrumentality of an Assembly and of a Council, with a permanent Secretariat.

ARTICLE 3. 1. The Assembly shall consist of Representatives of the Members of the League.

2. The Assembly shall meet at stated intervals and from time to time as occasion may require at the Seat of the League or at such other place as may be decided upon.

3. The Assembly may deal at its meetings with any matter within the sphere of action of the League or affecting the peace of the world.

4. At meetings of the Assembly, each Member of the League shall have one vote, and may have not more than three Representatives.

ARTICLE 4. 1. The Council shall consist of Representatives of the Principal Allied and Associated Powers, together with Representatives of four other Members of the League. These four Members of the League shall be selected by the Assembly from time to time in its discretion. Until the appointment of the Representatives of the four Members of the League first selected by the Assembly, Representatives of Belgium, Brazil, Spain and Greece shall be members of the Council.

2. With the approval of the majority of the Assembly, the Council may name additional Members of the League whose Representatives shall always be Members of the Council; the Council with like approval may increase the number of Members of the League to be selected by the Assembly for representation on the Council.

2bis. *The Assembly shall fix by a two-thirds majority the rules dealing with the election of the non-permanent Members of the Council, and particularly such regulations as relate to their term of office and the conditions of re-eligibility.*

3. The Council shall meet from time to time as occasion may require, and at least once a year, at the Seat of the League, or at such other place as may be decided upon.

4. The Council may deal at its meetings with any matter within the sphere of action of the League or affecting the peace of the world.

5. Any Member of the League not represented on the Council shall be invited to send a Representative to sit as a member at any meeting of the Council during the consideration of matters specially affecting the interests of that Member of the League.

6. At meetings of the Council, each Member of the League represented on the Council shall have one vote, and may have not more than one Representative.

ARTICLE 5. 1. Except where otherwise expressly provided in this Covenant or by the terms of the present Treaty, decisions at any meeting of the Assembly or of the Council shall require the agreement of all the Members of the League represented at the meeting.

2. All matters of procedure at meetings of the Assembly or of the Council, including the appointment of Committees to investigate particular matters shall be regulated by the Assembly or by the Council and may be decided by a majority of the Members of the League represented at the meeting.

3. The first meetings of the Assembly and the first meeting of the Council shall be summoned by the President of the United States of America.

ARTICLE 6. 1. The permanent Secretariat shall be established at the Seat of the League. The Secretariat shall comprise a Secretary-General and such secretaries and staff as may be required.

2. The first Secretary-General shall be the person named in the Annex; thereafter the Secretary-General shall be appointed by the Council with the approval of the majority of the Assembly.

3. The secretaries and staff of the Secretariat shall be appointed by the Secretary-General with the approval of the Council.

4. The Secretary-General shall act in that capacity at all meetings of the Assembly and of the Council.

5. *The expenses of the League shall be borne by the Members of the League in the proportion decided by the Assembly.*

ARTICLE 7. 1. The Seat of the League is established at Geneva.

2. The Council may at any time decide that the Seat of the League shall be established elsewhere.

3. All positions under or in connection with the League, including the Secretariat, shall be open equally to men and women.

4. Representatives of the Members of the League and officials of the League when engaged on the business of the League shall enjoy diplomatic privileges and immunities.

5. The buildings and other property occupied by the League or its officials or by Representatives attending its meetings shall be inviolable.

ARTICLE 8. 1. The Members of the League recognise that the maintenance of peace requires the reduction of national armaments to the lowest point consistent with national safety and the enforcement by common action of international obligations.

2. The Council, taking account of the geographical situation and circumstances of each State, shall formulate plans for such reduction for the consideration and action of the several Governments.

3. Such plans shall be subject to reconsideration and revision at least every ten years.

4. After these plans shall have been adopted by the several Governments, the limits of armaments therein fixed shall not be exceeded without the concurrence of the Council.

5. The Members of the League agree that the manufacture by private enterprise of munitions and implements of war is open to grave objections. The Council shall advise how the evil effects attendant upon such manufacture can be prevented, due regard being had to the necessities of those Members of the League which are not able to manufacture the munitions and implements of war necessary for their safety.

6. The Members of the League undertake to interchange full and frank information as to the scale of their armaments, their military, naval and air programmes and the conditions of such of their industries as are adaptable to warlike purposes.

ARTICLE 9. A permanent Commission shall be constituted to advise the Council on the execution of the provisions of Articles 1 and 8 and on military, naval and air questions generally.

ARTICLE 10. The Members of the League undertake to respect and preserve as against external aggression the territorial integrity and existing political independence of all Members of the League. In case of any such aggression or in case of any threat or danger of such aggression the Council shall advise upon the means by which this obligation shall be fulfilled.

ARTICLE 11. 1. Any war or threat of war, whether immediately affecting any of the Members of the League or not, is hereby declared a matter of concern to the whole League, and the League shall take any action that may be deemed wise and effectual to safeguard the peace of nations. In case any such emergency should arise the Secretary-General shall on the request of any Member of the League forthwith summon a meeting of the Council.

2. It is also declared to be the friendly right of each Member of the League to bring to the attention of the Assembly or of the Council any circumstance whatever affecting international relations which threatens to disturb international peace or the good understanding between nations upon which peace depends.

ARTICLE 12. 1. The Members of the League agree that if there should arise between them any dispute likely to lead to a rupture they will submit the matter either to arbitration *or judicial settlement* or to enquiry by the Council, and they agree in no case to resort to war until three months after the award by the arbitrators *or the judicial decision* or the report by the Council.

2. In any case under this Article the award of the arbitrators *or the judicial decision* shall be made within a reasonable time, and the report of the Council shall be made within six months after the submission of the dispute.

ARTICLE 13. 1. The Members of the League agree that whenever any dispute shall arise between them which they recognise to be suitable for submission to arbitration *or judicial settlement,* and which cannot be satisfactorily settled by diplomacy, they will submit the whole subject-matter to arbitration *or judicial settlement.*

2. Disputes as to the interpretation of a treaty, as to any question of international law, as to the existence of any fact which, if established would constitute a breach of any international obligation, or as to the extent and nature of the reparation to be made for any such breach, are declared to be among those which are generally suitable for submission to arbitration *or judicial settlement.*

3. *For the consideration of any such dispute, the court to which the case is referred shall be the Permanent Court of International Justice, established in accordance with Article* 14, *or any tribunal agreed on by the parties to the dispute or stipulated in any convention existing between them.*

4. The Members of the League agree that they will carry out in full good faith any award *or decision* that may be rendered, and that they will not resort to war against a Member of the League which complies therewith. In the event of any failure to carry out such an award *or decision,* the Council shall propose what steps should be taken to give effect thereto.

ARTICLE 14. The Council shall formulate and submit to the Members of the League for adoption plans for the establishment of a Permanent Court of International Justice. The Court shall be competent to hear and determine any dispute of an international character which the parties thereto submit to it. The Court may also give an advisory opinion upon any dispute or question referred to it by the Council or by the Assembly.

ARTICLE 15. 1. If there should arise between Members of the League any dispute likely to lead to a rupture, which is not submitted to arbitration *or judicial settlement* in accordance with Article 13, the Members of the League agree that they will submit the matter to the Council. Any party to the dispute may effect such submission by giving notice of the existence of the dispute to the Secretary-General, who will make all necessary arrangements for a full investigation and consideration thereof.

2. For this purpose the parties to the dispute will communicate to the Secretary-General, as promptly as

possible, statements of their case with all the relevant facts and papers, and the Council may forthwith direct the publication thereof.

3. The Council shall endeavour to effect a settlement of the dispute, and if such efforts are successful, a statement shall be made public giving such facts and explanations regarding the dispute and the terms of settlement thereof as the Council may deem appropriate.

4. If the dispute is not thus settled, the Council either unanimously or by a majority vote shall make and publish a report containing a statement of the facts of the dispute and the recommendations which are deemed just and proper in regard thereto.

5. Any Member of the League represented on the Council may make public a statement of the facts of the dispute and of its conclusions regarding the same.

6. If a report by the Council is unanimously agreed to by the members thereof other than the Representatives of one or more of the parties to the dispute, the Members of the League agree that they will not go to war with any party to the dispute which complies with the recommendations of the report.

7. If the Council fails to reach a report which is unanimously agreed to by the members thereof, other than the Representatives of one or more of the parties to the dispute, the Members of the League reserve to themselves the right to take such action as they shall consider necessary for the maintenance of right and justice.

8. If the dispute between the parties is claimed by one of them, and is found by the Council, to arise out of a matter which by international law is solely within the domestic jurisdiction of that party, the Council shall so report, and shall make no recommendation as to its settlement.

9. The Council may in any case under this Article refer the dispute to the Assembly. The dispute shall be so referred at the request of either party to the dispute provided that such request be made within fourteen days after the submission of the dispute to the Council.

10. In any case referred to the Assembly, all the provisions of this Article and of Article 12 relating to the action and powers of the Council shall apply to the action

and powers of the Assembly, provided that a report made by the Assembly, if concurred in by the Representatives of those Members of the League represented on the Council and of a majority of the other Members of the League, exclusive in each case of the Representatives of the parties to the dispute, shall have the same force as a report by the Council concurred in by all the members thereof other than the Representative of one or more of the parties to the dispute.

ARTICLE 16. 1. Should any Member of the League resort to war in disregard of its covenants under Articles 12, 13 or 15, it shall *ipso facto* be deemed to have committed an act of war against all other Members of the League, which hereby undertake immediately to subject it to the severance of all trade or financial relations, the prohibition of all intercourse between their nationals and the nationals of the covenant-breaking State, and the prevention of all financial, commercial or personal intercourse between the nationals of the covenant-breaking State and the nationals of any other State, whether a Member of the League or not.

2. It shall be the duty of the Council in such case to recommend to the several Governments concerned what effective military, naval or air force the Members of the League shall severally contribute to the armed forces to be used to protect the covenants of the League.

3. The Members of the League agree, further, that they will mutually support one another in the financial and economic measures which are taken under this Article, in order to minimise the loss and inconvenience resulting from the above measures, and that they will mutually support one another in resisting any special measures aimed at one of their number by the covenant-breaking State, and that they will take the necessary steps to afford passage through their territory to the forces of any of the Members of the League which are coöperating to protect the covenants of the League.

4. Any Member of the League which has violated any covenant of the League may be declared to be no longer a Member of the League by a vote of the Council concurred in by the Representatives of all the other Members of the League represented thereon.

ARTICLE 17. 1. In the event of a dispute between a Member of the League and a State which is not a Member of the League, or between States not Members of the League, the State or States not Members of the League shall be invited to accept the obligations of membership in the League for the purposes of such dispute, upon such conditions as the Council may deem just. If such invitation is accepted, the provisions of Articles 12 to 16 inclusive shall be applied with such modifications as may be deemed necessary by the Council.

2. Upon such invitation being given the Council shall immediately institute an inquiry into the circumstances of the dispute and recommend such action as may seem best and most effectual in the circumstances.

3. If a State so invited shall refuse to accept the obligations of membership in the League for the purposes of such dispute, and shall resort to war against a Member of the League, the provisions of Article 16 shall be applicable as against the State taking such action.

4. If both parties to the dispute when so invited refuse to accept the obligations of membership in the League for the purposes of such dispute, the Council may take such measures and make such recommendations as will prevent hostilities and will result in the settlement of the dispute.

ARTICLE 18. Every treaty or international engagement entered into hereafter by any Member of the League shall be forthwith registered with the Secretariat and shall as soon as possible be published by it. No such treaty or international engagement shall be binding until so registered.

ARTICLE 19. The Assembly may from time to time advise the reconsideration by Members of the League of treaties which have become inapplicable and the consideration of international conditions whose continuance might endanger the peace of the world.

ARTICLE 20. 1. The Members of the League severally agree that this Covenant is accepted as abrogating all obligations or understandings *inter se* which are inconsistent with the terms thereof, and solemnly undertake that they will not hereafter enter into any engagements inconsistent with the terms thereof.

2. In case any Member of the League shall, before becoming a Member of the League, have undertaken any obligations inconsistent with the terms of this Covenant, it shall be the duty of such Member to take immediate steps to procure its release from such obligations.

ARTICLE 21. Nothing in this Covenant shall be deemed to affect the validity of international engagements, such as treaties of arbitration or regional understandings like the Monroe Doctrine, for securing the maintenance of peace.

ARTICLE 22. 1. To those colonies and territories which as a consequence of the late war have ceased to be under the sovereignty of the States which formerly governed them and which are inhabited by peoples not yet able to stand by themselves under the strenuous conditions of the modern world, there should be applied the principle that the well-being and development of such peoples form a sacred trust of civilisation and that securities for the performance of this trust should be embodied in this Covenant.

2. The best method of giving practical effect to this principle is that the tutelage of such peoples should be entrusted to advanced nations who by reason of their resources, their experience or their geographical position can best undertake this responsibility, and who are willing to accept it, and that this tutelage should be exercised by them as Mandatories on behalf of the League.

3. The character of the mandate must differ according to the stage of the development of the people, the geographical situation of the territory, its economic conditions and other similar circumstances.

4. Certain communities formerly belonging to the Turkish Empire have reached a stage of development where their existence as independent nations can be provisionally recognised subject to the rendering of administrative advice and assistance by a Mandatory until such time as they are able to stand alone. The wishes of these communities must be a principal consideration in the selection of the Mandatory.

5. Other peoples, especially those of Central Africa, are at such a stage that the Mandatory must be responsible for the administration of the territory under conditions

which will guarantee freedom of conscience and religion, subject only to the maintenance of public order and morals, the prohibition of abuses such as the slave trade, the arms traffic and the liquor traffic, and the prevention of the establishment of fortifications or military and naval bases and of military training of the natives for other than police purposes and the defence of territory, and will also secure equal opportunities for the trade and commerce of other Members of the League.

6. There are territories, such as South-West Africa and certain of the South Pacific Islands, which, owing to the sparseness of their population, or their small size, or their remoteness from the centres of civilisation, or their geographical contiguity to the territory of the Mandatory, and other circumstances, can be best administered under the laws of the Mandatory as integral portions of its territory, subject to the safeguards above mentioned in the interest of the indigenous population.

7. In every case of mandate, the Mandatory shall render to the Council an annual report in reference to the territory committed to its charge.

8. The degree of authority, control or administration to be exercised by the Mandatory shall, if not previously agreed upon by the Members of the League, be explicitly defined in each case by the Council.

9. A permanent Commission shall be constituted to receive and examine the annual reports of the Mandatories and to advise the Council on all matters relating to the observance of the mandates.

ARTICLE 23. Subject to and in accordance with the provisions of international conventions existing or hereafter to be agreed upon, the Members of the League:

(a) will endeavour to secure and maintain fair and humane conditions of labour for men, women, and children, both in their own countries and in all countries to which commercial and industrial relations extend, and for that purpose will establish and maintain the necessary international organisations;

(b) undertake to secure just treatment of the native inhabitants of territories under their control;

(c) will entrust the League with the general supervision over the execution of agreements with regard to the traffic in women and children, and the traffic in opium and other dangerous drugs;

(d) will entrust the League with the general supervision of the trade in arms and ammunitions with the countries in which the control of this traffic is necessary in the common interest;

(e) will make provision to secure and maintain freedom of communications and of transit and equitable treatment for the commerce of all Members of the League. In this connection, the special necessities of the regions devastated during the war of 1914-1918 shall be borne in mind;

(f) will endeavour to take steps in matters of international concern for the prevention and control of disease.

ARTICLE 24. 1. There shall be placed under the direction of the League all international bureaux already established by general treaties if the parties to such treaties consent. All such international bureaux and all commissions for the regulation of matters of international interest hereafter constituted shall be placed under the direction of the League.

2. In all matters of international interest which are regulated by general conventions but which are not placed under the control of international bureaux or commissions, the Secretariat of the League shall, subject to the consent of the Council and if desired by the parties, collect and distribute all relevant information and shall render any other assistance which may be necessary or desirable.

3. The Council may include as part of the expenses of the Secretariat the expenses of any bureau or commission which is placed under the direction of the League.

ARTICLE 25. The Members of the League agree to encourage and promote the establishment and coöperation of duly authorised voluntary national Red Cross organisations having as purposes the improvement of health, the prevention of disease and the mitigation of suffering throughout the world.

ARTICLE 26. 1. Amendments to this Covenant will

take effect when ratified by the Members of the League whose Representatives compose the Council and by a majority of the Members of the League whose Representatives compose the Assembly.

2. No such amendments shall bind any Member of the League which signifies its dissent therefrom but in that case it shall cease to be a Member of the League.

ANNEX

I. Original Members of the League of Nations Signatories of the Treaty of Peace

United States of America,* Belgium, Bolivia, Brazil, British Empire, (Canada, Australia, South Africa, New Zealand, India), China, Cuba, Ecuador, France, Greece, Guatemala, Haiti, Hedjaz, Honduras, Italy, Japan, Liberia, Nicaragua, Panama, Peru, Poland, Portugal, Roumania, Serb-Croat-Slovene State, Siam, Czecho-Slovakia, Uruguay.

States Invited to Accede to the Covenant

Argentine Republic, Chile, Colombia, Denmark, Netherlands, Norway, Paraguay, Persia, Salvador, Spain, Sweden, Switzerland, Venezuela.

II. First Secretary General of League of Nations

The Honourable Sir James Eric Drummond, K.C.M.G., C.B.

---

* Although mentioned as an "original member," the United States subsequently refused to accept membership in the League of Nations.

EXTRACTS FROM THE TREATY OF VERSAILLES, JUNE 28, 1919[10]

The Treaty of Versailles, between the Allies and Germany, was signed in the Hall of Mirrors in the palace of Versailles on June 28, 1919. Both the time and the place were selected to humiliate Germany—the time was the fifth anniversary of the assassination at Sarajevo, and the place was the same hall where, in 1871, the German Empire had been proclaimed. The treaty was ratified by the signatories in Paris on January 10, 1920. The entire document, composed of 15 parts, 440 articles, and almost a score of annexes, is too lengthy to be reproduced in full here. Following are the more important articles.

✔   ✔   ✔

PART II

Boundaries of Germany [Omitted]

PART III

Political Clauses for Europe

ARTICLE 31. Germany, recognizing that the Treaties of April 19, 1839, which established the status of Belgium before the war, no longer conform to the requirements of the situation, consents to the abrogation of the said treaties and undertakes immediately to recognize and to observe whatever conventions may be entered into by the Principal Allied and Associated Powers, or by any of them, in concert with the Governments of Belgium and of the Netherlands, to replace the said Treaties of 1839. If her formal adhesion should be required to such con-

---

[10] United States, 66th Congress, 1st Session, Senate Document No. 49, *Treaty of Peace with Germany* (Washington, 1919).

ventions or to any of their stipulations, Germany undertakes immediately to give it.

ARTICLE 42. Germany is forbidden to maintain or construct any fortifications either on the left bank of the Rhine or on the right bank to the west of a line drawn 50 kilometres to the East of the Rhine.

ARTICLE 43. In the area defined above the maintenance and the assembly of armed forces, either permanently or temporarily, and military manœuvres of any kind, as well as the upkeep of all permanent works for mobilization, are in the same way forbidden.

ARTICLE 44. In case Germany violates in any manner whatever the provisions of Articles 42 and 43, she shall be regarded as committing a hostile act against the Powers signatory of the present Treaty and as calculated to disturb the peace of the world.

ARTICLE 45. As compensation for the destruction of the coal-mines in the north of France and as part payment towards the total reparation due from Germany for the damage resulting from the war, Germany cedes to France in full and absolute possession, with exclusive rights of exploitation, unencumbered and free from all debts and charges of any kind, the coal-mines situated in the Saar Basin as defined in Article 48.

ARTICLE 46. In order to assure the rights and welfare of the population and to guarantee to France complete freedom in working the mines, Germany agrees to the provisions of Chapters I and II of the Annex hereto.

ARTICLE 49. Germany renounces in favour of the League of Nations, in the capacity of trustee, the government of the territory defined above.

ARTICLE 50. The stipulations under which the cession of the mines in the Saar Basin shall be carried out, together with the measures intended to guarantee the rights and the well-being of the inhabitants and the government of the territory, as well as the conditions in accordance with which the plebiscite hereinbefore provided for is to be made, are laid down in the Annex hereto. This Annex shall be considered as an integral part of the present Treaty, and Germany declares her adherence to it.

ARTICLE 51. The territories which were ceded to

Germany in accordance with the Preliminaries of Peace signed at Versailles on February 26, 1871, and the Treaty of Frankfurt of May 10, 1871, are restored to French sovereignty as from the date of the Armistice of November 11, 1918.

The provisions of the Treaties establishing the delimitation of the frontiers before 1871 shall be restored.

ARTICLE 80. Germany acknowledges and will respect strictly the independence of Austria, within the frontiers which may be fixed in a Treaty between that State and the Principal Allied and Associated Powers; she agrees that this independence shall be inalienable, except with the consent of the Council of the League of Nations.

ARTICLE 81. Germany, in conformity with the action already taken by the Allied and Associated Powers, recognizes the complete independence of the Czecho-Slovak State which will include the autonomous territory of the Ruthenians to the south of the Carpathians. Germany hereby recognizes the frontiers of this State as determined by the Principal Allied and Associated Powers and the other interested States.

ARTICLE 87. Germany, in conformity with the action already taken by the Allied and Associated Powers, recognizes the complete independence of Poland, and renounces in her favour all rights and title over the territory [of Poland].

The boundaries of Poland not laid down in the present Treaty will be subsequently determined by the Principal Allied and Associated Powers.

A Commission consisting of seven members, five of whom shall be nominated by the Principal Allied and Associated Powers, one by Germany and one by Poland, shall be constituted fifteen days after the coming into force of the present Treaty to delimit on the spot the frontier line between Poland and Germany.

The decisions of the Commission will be taken by a majority of votes and shall be binding upon the parties concerned.

ARTICLE 88. In the portion of Upper Silesia included within the boundaries described below, the inhabitants will be called upon to indicate by a vote whether they wish to be attached to Germany or to Poland. . . .

ARTICLE 99. Germany renounces in favour of the Principal Allied and Associated Powers all rights and title over the territories included between the Baltic, the north-eastern frontier of East Prussia as defined in Article 28 of Part II (Boundaries of Germany) of the present Treaty and the former frontier between Germany and Russia.

Germany undertakes to accept the settlement made by the Principal Allied and Associated Powers in regard to these territories, particularly in so far as concerns the nationality of the inhabitants.

ARTICLE 101. A Commission composed of three members appointed by the Principal Allied and Associated Powers, including a High Commissioner as President, one member appointed by Germany and one member appointed by Poland, shall be constituted within fifteen days of the coming into force of the present Treaty for the purpose of delimiting on the spot the frontier of the territory as described above, taking into account as far as possible the existing communal boundaries.

ARTICLE 102. The Principal Allied and Associated Powers undertake to establish the town of Danzig, together with the rest of the territory described in Article 100, as a Free City. It will be placed under the protection of the League of Nations.

PART IV

German Rights and Interests Outside Germany

ARTICLE 119. Germany renounces in favour of the Principal Allied and Associated Powers all her rights and titles over her oversea possessions.

ARTICLE 141. Germany renounces all rights, titles and privileges conferred on her by the General Act of Algeciras of April 7, 1906, and by the Franco-German Agreements of February 9, 1909, and November 4, 1911. All treaties, agreements, arrangements and contracts concluded by her with the Sherifian Empire are regarded as abrogated as from August 3, 1914.

In no case can Germany take advantage of these instruments and she undertakes not to intervene in any way in negotiations relating to Morocco which may take place between France and the other Powers.

ARTICLE 156. Germany renounces, in favour of Japan, all her rights, title and privileges—particularly those concerning the territory of Kiaochow, railways, mines and submarine cables—which she acquired in virtue of the Treaty concluded by her with China on March 6, 1898, and of all other arrangements relative to the Province of Shantung.

All German rights in the Tsingtao-Tsinanfu Railway, including its branch lines, together with its subsidiary property of all kinds, stations, shops, fixed and rolling stock, mines, plant and material for the exploitation of the mines, are and remain acquired by Japan, together with all rights and privileges attaching thereto.

The German State submarine cables from Tsingtao to Shanghai and from Tsingtao to Chefoo, with all the rights, privileges and properties attaching thereto, are similarly acquired by Japan, free and clear of all charges and encumbrances.

PART V

Military, Naval, and Air Claims

ARTICLE 159. The German military forces shall be demobilized and reduced as prescribed hereinafter.

ARTICLE 160. By a date which must not be later than March 31, 1920, the German Army must not comprise more than seven divisions of infantry and three divisions of cavalry.

After that date the total number of effectives in the Army of the States constituting Germany must not exceed one hundred thousand men, including officers and establishments of depots. The Army shall be devoted exclusively to the maintenance of order within the territory and to the control of the frontiers.

The total effective strength of officers, including the personnel of staffs, whatever their composition, must not exceed four thousand.

. . . The Great German General Staff and all similar organizations shall be dissolved and may not be reconstituted in any form.

ARTICLE 189. All fortified works, fortresses and field works situated in German territory to the west of a line drawn fifty kilometres to the east of the Rhine shall be disarmed and dismantled.

ARTICLE 181. After the expiration of a period of two months from the coming into force of the present Treaty the German naval forces in commission must not exceed:

6 battleships of the *Deutschland* or *Lothringen* type,
6 light cruisers,
12 destroyers,
12 torpedo boats,

or an equal number of ships constructed to replace them as provided in Article 190.

No submarines are to be included.

All other warships, except where there is provision to the contrary in the present Treaty, must be placed in reserve or devoted to commercial purposes.

ARTICLE 198. The armed forces of Germany must not include any military or naval air forces.

PART VI

Reparation

ARTICLE 231. The Allied and Associated Governments affirm and Germany accepts the responsibility of Germany and her allies for causing all the loss and damage to which the Allied and Associated Governments and their nationals have been subjected as a consequence of the war imposed upon them by the aggression of Germany and her allies.

ARTICLE 232. The Allied and Associated Governments recognize that the resources of Germany are not adequate, after taking into account permanent diminutions of such resources which will result from other provisions of the present Treaty, to make complete reparation for all such loss and damage.

The Allied and Associated Governments, however, require, and Germany undertakes, that she will make compensation for all damage done to the civilian population of the Allied and Associated Powers and to their property during the period of the belligerency of each as an Allied or Associated Power against Germany by such aggression by land, by sea and from the air, and in general all damage as defined in Annex I hereto.

ARTICLE 233. The amount of the above damage for which compensation is to be made by Germany shall be determined by an Inter-Allied Commission, to be called the *Reparation Commission* and constituted in the form and with the powers set forth hereunder and in Annexes II to VII inclusive hereto.

This Commission shall consider the claims and give to the German Government a just opportunity to be heard.

The findings of the Commission as to the amount of damage defined as above shall be concluded and notified to the German Government on or before May 1, 1921, as representing the extent of that Government's obligations.

ARTICLE 234. The Reparation Commission shall after May 1, 1921, from time to time, consider the resources and capacity of Germany, and, after giving her representatives a just opportunity to be heard, shall have discretion to extend the date, and to modify the form of payments, such as are to be provided for in accordance with Article 233; but not to cancel any part, except with the specific authority of the several Governments represented upon the Commission.

PART X

Special Provisions

ARTICLE 245. Within six months after the coming into force of the present Treaty the German Government must restore to the French Government the trophies, archives, historical souvenirs or works of art carried away from France by the German authorities in the course of the war of 1870-1871 and during this last war, in accordance with a list which will be communicated to it by the French Government; particularly the French flags taken in the course of the war of 1870-1871 and all the political papers taken by the German authorities on October 10, 1870, at the château of Cerçay, near Brunoy (Seine-et-Oise) belonging at the time to Mr. Rouher, formerly Minister of State.

ARTICLE 246. Within six months from the coming into force of the present Treaty, Germany will restore to His Majesty the King of the Hedjaz the original Koran of the Caliph Othman, which was removed from Medina by the Turkish authorities and is stated to have been presented to the ex-Emperor William II.

Within the same period Germany will hand over to His Britannic Majesty's Government the skull of the Sultan Mkwawa which was removed from the Protectorate of German East Africa and taken to Germany.

PART XIV

Guarantees

ARTICLE 428. As a guarantee for the execution of the present Treaty by Germany, the German territory situated to the west of the Rhine, together with the bridgeheads, will be occupied by Allied and Associated troops for a period of fifteen years from the coming into force of the present Treaty.

ARTICLE 431. If before the expiration of the period of fifteen years Germany complies with all the undertakings resulting from the present Treaty, the occupying forces will be withdrawn immediately.

ARTICLE 48 OF THE WEIMAR CONSTITUTION, AUGUST 11, 1919[11]

The Weimar Constitution of the postwar German Republic was considered to be one of the most advanced democratic documents in history. Unfortunately, its effect was diminished if not destroyed by the following Article 48, which was used by Hitler in his "legal" liquidation of German democracy.

✓   ✓   ✓

ARTICLE 48. If a Land fails to fulfil the duties incumbent upon it according to the Constitution or the laws of the Reich, the Reich President can force it to do so with the help of the armed forces.

The Reich President may, if the public safety and order in the German Reich are considerably disturbed or endangered, take such measures as are necessary to restore public safety and order. If necessary he may intervene with the help of the armed forces. For this purpose he may temporarily suspend, either partially or wholly, the Fundamental Rights established in Articles 114, 115, 117, 118, 123, 124 and 153.

The Reich President shall inform the Reichstag without delay of all measures taken under Paragraph 1 or

[11] *Die Verfassung des Deutschen Reiches von 11. August, 1919* (Reclams Universal Bibliothek, No. 6051, Leipzig, 1930), pp. 17-18. The other articles mentioned in Article 48: Article 114 (freedom of the individual) ; Article 115 (freedom of residence) ; Article 117 (secrecy of postal, telegraph, and telephone communications) ; Article 118 (freedom of expression) ; Article 123 (freedom of assembly) ; Article 124 (freedom of organization) ; and 153 (personal property guarantee).

Paragraph 2 of this Article. On demand by the Reichstag the measures shall be repealed . . .

— 12 —

THE ENFRANCHISEMENT OF WOMEN IN GREAT BRITAIN AND THE UNITED STATES, 1918–1919

In recognition of the services rendered by women in World War I, the British Parliament enfranchised women by two acts in 1918 and 1928. In the United States, Article 19, or the 19th Amendment to the Constitution, granted nationwide suffrage to women.

✓   ✓   ✓

I

The British Act of February 6, 1918 [12]

4. A woman shall be entitled to be registered as a parliamentary elector for a constituency . . . if she—(a) has attained the age of thirty years; and (b) is not subject to any legal incapacity; and (c) is entitled to be registered as a local government elector in respect of the occupation in that constituency of land or premises (not being a dwelling house) of a yearly value of not less than five pounds or of a dwelling-house, or is the wife of a husband entitled to be so registered.

[12] *The Public General Statutes of Great Britain, 1917-18* (London, 1918), p. 255.

II

The British Act of July 2, 1928 [13]

1. For the purpose of providing that the parliamentary franchise shall be the same for men and women, subsections (1) and (2) of section four of the Representation of the People Act, 1918 . . . shall be repealed and the following section shall be substituted for sections (1) and (2) of that Act:

(1) A person shall be entitled to be registered as a parliamentary elector for a constituency . . . if he or she is of full age [21] and not subject to any legal incapacity; and (a) has the requisite residence qualification; or (b) has the requisite business premises qualification; or (c) is the husband or wife of a person entitled to be so registered in respect of a business premises qualification.

III

The 19th Amendment to the Constitution of the United States August 26, 1920 [14]

1. The right of citizens of the United States to vote shall not be denied or abridged by the United States on account of sex.

2. Congress shall have power, by appropriate legislation, to enforce the provisions of this article.

[13] *The Public General Acts of Great Britain, 1928* (London, 1928), p. 28.

[14] The amendment was proposed to the Legislatures of the several States by the 65th Congress, having been adopted by the House of Representatives, May 21, 1919, and by the Senate, June 4, 1919. On August 26, 1920 this amendment was proclaimed in effect, having been adopted by three-quarters of the States. The Tennessee House, August 31, rescinded its ratification, 47 to 24.

— 13 —

THE 25-POINT PROGRAM OF THE NATIONAL SOCIALIST GERMAN WORKERS' PARTY, FEBRUARY 25, 1920[15]

The original program of the National Socialist German Workers' Party envisaged a "Third Reich" and a Greater Germany. The catchwords of the movement were anti-Semitism and anti-Bolshevism.

✦ ✦ ✦

The program of the German Workers' Party is limited as to period. The leaders have no intention, once the aims announced in it have been achieved, of setting up fresh ones, merely in order to increase the discontent of the masses artificially and so ensure the continued existence of the party.

1. We demand the union of all Germans to form a Great Germany on the basis of the right of self-determination of nations.

2. We demand equality of rights for the German people in its dealings with other nations, and abolition of the Peace Treaties of Versailles and Saint-Germain.

3. We demand land and territory [colonies] for the nourishment of our people and for settling our surplus population.

4. None but members of the nation [*Volksgenossen*] may be citizens of the State. None but those of German blood, whatever their creed, may be members of the nation. No Jew, therefore, may be a member of the nation.

5. Any one who is not a citizen of the State may live

---

[15] *The Program of the National Socialist Workers' Party* (Munich, 1920).

in Germany only as a guest and must be subject to laws for aliens.

6. The right of voting for the leaders and laws of the State is to be enjoyed by the citizen of the State alone. We demand therefore that all official appointments, of whatever kind, whether in the Reich, in the Länder, or in the smaller localities, shall be granted to citizens of the State alone.

We oppose the corrupting custom of Parliament of filling posts merely with a view of party considerations, and without reference to character or capability.

7. We demand that the State shall make it its first duty to promote the industry and livelihood of citizens of the State. If it is not possible to nourish the entire population of the State, foreign nationals [non-citizens] must be excluded from the Reich.

8. All further non-German immigration must be prevented. We demand that all non-Germans who entered Germany subsequent to August 2nd, 1914, shall be compelled forthwith to depart from the Reich.

9. All citizens of the State shall be equal as regards rights and duties.

10. It must be the first duty of each citizen of the State to work with his mind or with his body. The activities of the individual may not clash with the interests of the whole, but must proceed within the frame of the community and be for the general good.

We demand therefore:

11. Abolition of all incomes unearned by work.

12. In view of the enormous sacrifice of life and property demanded of a nation by every war, personal enrichment due to a war must be regarded as a crime against the nation. We demand therefore ruthless confiscation of all war gains.

13. We demand nationalization of all businesses which have been up to the present formed into companies [trusts].

14. We demand that all the profits from wholesale trade shall be shared out.

15. We demand extensive development of provision for old age.

16. We demand creation and maintenance of a healthy

middle class, immediate communalization of department stores, and their lease at a cheap rate to small traders, and extreme consideration for all small purveyors to the State, district authorities, and smaller localities.

17. We demand land reform suitable to our national requirements, passing of a law for confiscation without compensation of land for common purposes; abolition of interest on land loans, and prevention of all speculation in land.

18. We demand a ruthless struggle against those whose activities are injurious to the common interest. Common criminals against the nation, usurers, profiteers, etc., must be punished with death, whatever their creed or race.

19. We demand that the Roman Law, which serves the materialistic world order, shall be replaced by a German legal system.

20. With the aim of opening to every capable and industrious German the possibility of higher education and of thus obtaining advancement, the State must consider a thorough reconstruction of our national system of education. The curriculum of all educational establishments must be brought into line with the requirements of practical life. Comprehension of the State idea [civic training] must be the school objective, beginning with the first dawn of understanding in the pupil. We demand development of the gifted children of poor parents, whatever their class or occupation, at the expense of the State.

21. The State must see to raising the standard of health in the nation by protecting mothers and infants, prohibiting child labor, increasing bodily efficiency by obligatory gymnastics and sports laid down by law, and by extensive support of clubs engaged in the bodily development of the young.

22. We demand abolition of a paid army, and formation of a national army.

23. We demand legal warfare against conscious political lying and its dissemination in the press. In order to facilitate creation of a German national press we demand:

(a) that all editors and their co-workers on newspapers employing the German language must be members of the nation;

(b) that special permission from the State shall be necessary before non-German newspapers may appear. These must not be printed in the German language;

(c) that non-Germans shall be prohibited by law from participation financially in or influencing German newspapers, and that the penalty for contravention of the law shall be suppression of any such newspaper and immediate deportation of the non-German concerned in it.

It must be forbidden to publish papers which do not conduce to the national welfare. We demand legal prosecution of all tendencies in art and literature of a kind likely to disintegrate our life as a nation, and the suppression of institutions which militate against the requirements above mentioned.

24. We demand liberty for all religious denominations in the State, so far as they are not a danger to, and do not militate against the moral feelings of, the German race.

The party, as such, stands for positive Christianity, but does not bind itself in the matter of creed to any particular confession. It combats the Jewish-materialist spirit within us and without us and is convinced that our nation can only achieve permanent health from within on the principle:

25. That all the foregoing may be realized, we demand the creation of a strong central power of the State. Unquestioned authority of the politically centralized Parliament over the entire Reich and its organizations; and formation of Chambers for classes and occupations for the purpose of carrying out the general laws promulgated by the Reich in the various states of the confederation.

The leaders of the party swear to go straight forward —if necessary to sacrifice their lives—in securing fulfilment of the foregoing points.

— 14 —

THE ZINOVIEV LETTER, SEPTEMBER 15, 1924 [16]

The publication in *The London Times* of a letter said to have been written by Gregory Zinoviev, president of the Third International, to British Communists, seriously hurt the Labor Party in the elections of 1924. Soviet Russia branded the letter a forgery.

↗   ↗   ↗

Very Secret

To the Central Committee, British Communist Party

Executive Committee
Third Communist International
Presidium

Sept. 15, 1924, Moscow

Dear Comrades:

The time is approaching for the Parliament of England to consider the Treaty concluded between the Governments of Great Britain and the U.S.S.R. for the purpose of ratification. The fierce campaign raised by the British bourgeoisie around the question shows the majority of the same, together with reactionary circles, as against the Treaty for the purpose of breaking off an agreement consolidating the ties between the proletariats of the two countries leading to the restoration of normal relations between England and the U.S.S.R. . . .

. . . Organize a campaign of disclosure of the foreign policy of MacDonald. . . .

The IKKI [Executive Committee of the Third Communist International] will willingly place at your disposal the wide material in its possession regarding the activities of British Imperialism in the Middle and Far East. . . .

[16] *The Times,* London, October 25, 1924.

Armed warfare must be preceded by a struggle against the inclinations to compromise which are imbedded among the majority of British workmen, against the ideas of evolution and peaceful extermination of capitalism. Only then will it be possible to count upon complete success of an armed insurrection. . . .

. . . It would be desirable to have cells in all the units of the troops, particularly among those quartered in the large centres of the country, and also among the factories working on munitions and at military store depôts. . . .

In the event of danger of war, . . . it is possible to paralyze all military preparations of the bourgeoisie and make a start in turning an imperialist war into a class war. . . .

Desiring you all success, both in organization and in your struggle.

With Communist Greetings,
President of the Presidium of the IKKI
Zinoviev
Member of the Presidium
McManus
Secretary Kuusinen

THE LOCARNO PACT, OCTOBER 16, 1925 [17]

The peace agreements made at the famous conference at Locarno, Switzerland, in 1925, were hailed at the time as a milestone on the road to permanent peace. Locarno became a temporary symbol of "sweetness and light" in international relations.

✓   ✓   ✓

The President of the German Reich, His Majesty the King of the Belgians, the President of the French Republic, His Majesty the King of the United Kingdom of Great Britain and Ireland and of the British Dominions beyond the Seas, Emperor of India, and His Majesty the King of Italy;

Anxious to satisfy the desire for security and protection which animates the peoples upon whom fell the scourge of the war of 1914-1918;

Taking note of the abrogation of the treaties for the neutralisation of Belgium, and conscious of the necessity of ensuring peace in the area which has so frequently been the scene of European conflicts;

Animated also with the sincere desire of giving to all the signatory Powers concerned supplementary guarantees within the framework of the Covenant of the League of Nations and the treaties in force between them;

Have determined to conclude a treaty with these objects, and have appointed as their plenipotentiaries:

[*Names of Plenipotentiaries*]

Who, having communicated their full powers, found in good and due form, have agreed as follows:—

[17] League of Nations, *Treaty Series, 1926-1927,* LIV, pp. 291-97: Treaty of Mutual Guarantee between Germany, Belgium, France, Great Britain, and Italy, October 16, 1925.

ARTICLE 1. The High Contracting Parties collectively and severally guarantee, in the manner provided in the following Articles, the maintenance of the territorial *status quo* resulting from the frontiers between Germany and Belgium and between Germany and France, and the inviolability of the said frontiers as fixed by or in pursuance of the Treaty of Peace signed at Versailles on June 28, 1919, and also the observance of the stipulations of Articles 42 and 43 of the said treaty concerning the demilitarised zone.

ARTICLE 2. Germany and Belgium, and also Germany and France, mutually undertake that they will in no case attack or invade each other or resort to war against each other.

This stipulation shall not, however, apply in the case of:

1. The exercise of the right of legitimate defence, that is to say, resistance to a violation of the undertaking contained in the previous paragraph or to a flagrant breach of Articles 42 or 43 of the said Treaty of Versailles, if such breach constitutes an unprovoked act of aggression and by reason of the assembly of armed forces in the demilitarised zone immediate action is necessary;
2. Action in pursuance of Article 16 of the Covenant of the League of Nations;
3. Action as the result of a decision taken by the Assembly or by the Council of the League of Nations or in pursuance of Article 15, paragraph 7, of the Covenant of the League of Nations, provided that in this last event the action is directed against a State which was the first to attack.

ARTICLE 3. In view of the undertakings entered into in Article 2 of the present Treaty, Germany and Belgium, and Germany and France, undertake to settle by peaceful means and in the manner laid down herein all questions of every kind which may arise between them and which it may not be possible to settle by the normal methods of diplomacy:

Any question with regard to which the Parties are in

conflict as to their respective rights shall be submitted to judicial decision, and the Parties undertake to comply with such decision.

All other questions shall be submitted to a conciliation commission. If the proposals of this commission are not accepted by the two Parties, the question shall be brought before the Council of the League of Nations, which will deal with it in accordance with Article 15 of the Covenant of the League.

The detailed arrangements for effecting such peaceful settlement are the subject of special Agreements signed this day.

ARTICLE 4. (1) If one of the High Contracting Parties alleges that a violation of Article 2 of the present Treaty or a breach of Articles 42 or 43 of the Treaty of Versailles has been or is being committed, it shall bring the question at once before the Council of the League of Nations. . . .

ARTICLE 7. The present Treaty, which is designed to ensure the maintenance of peace, and is in conformity with the Covenant of the League of Nations, shall not be interpreted as restricting the duty of the League to take whatever action may be deemed wise and effectual to safeguard the peace of the world.

ARTICLE 8. The present Treaty shall be registered at the League of Nations in accordance with the Covenant of the League. It shall remain in force until the Council, acting on a request of one or other of the High Contracting Parties notified to the other signatory Powers three months in advance, and voting at least by a two-thirds' majority, decides that the League of Nations ensures sufficient protection to the High Contracting Parties; the Treaty shall cease to have effect on the expiration of a period of one year from such decision.

ARTICLE 9. The present Treaty shall impose no obligation upon any of the British dominions, or upon India, unless the Government of such dominion, or of India, signifies its acceptance thereof.

ARTICLE 10. The present Treaty shall be ratified and the ratifications shall be deposited at Geneva in the archives of the League of Nations as soon as possible.

It shall enter into force as soon as all the ratifications have been deposited and Germany has become a Member of the League of Nations.

The present Treaty, done in a single copy, will be deposited in the archives of the League of Nations, and the Secretary-General will be requested to transmit certified copies to each of the High Contracting Parties.

In faith whereof the above-mentioned Plenipotentiaries have signed the present Treaty.

Done at Locarno, October 16, 1925

— 16 —

THE TANAKA MEMORIAL, JULY 25, 1927 [18]

In 1927 Premier Baron Gi-ichi Tanaka was said to have placed before the Japanese Emperor a blueprint for world conquest. Released through Chinese sources, the Tanaka Memorial was denounced by the Japanese as a forgery. Forged or not, it exerted a tremendous influence in the Far East. Following are the two key paragraphs.

✓   ✓   ✓

For her self-protection as well as for the protection of others, Japan cannot remove the difficulties in Eastern Asia unless she adopts a policy of blood-and-iron. However, in implementing this policy we must face the United States, which has been turned against us by China's policy of fighting poison with poison. If we want to control China in the future, we must first crush the United

[18] *The Tanaka Memorial* (1927).

States, just as in past times we have had to fight in the
Russo-Japanese War. To conquer China we must first
overwhelm Manchuria and Mongolia. To conquer the
world, we must first conquer China. If we are successful
in conquering China, the remainder of the Asiatic nations
and the South Sea countries will fear and surrender to
us. Only then will the world admit that Eastern Asia is
ours and will not dare to challenge our rights. This is
the plan bequeathed to us by our Emperor Meijii, the
success of which is necessary for our national existence. . . .

The method of gaining actual rights in Manchuria and
Mongolia is to use this area as a base and, while pre-
tending trade and commerce, penetrate the rest of China.
With these rights secured, we shall seize the resources of
all the country. And with China's resources at our disposal, we shall then conquer India, the Archipelago, Asia
Minor, Central Asia, and even Europe. The first step,
however, is to obtain control of Manchuria and Mongolia,
if our Yamato race desires to distinguish itself on Con-
tinental Asia.

— 17 —

THE KELLOGG-BRIAND PACT FOR THE RENUNCIATION OF WAR, AUGUST 27, 1928 [19]

The Kellogg-Briand Pact, resulting from a correspond-
ence between Briand, the French Foreign Minister, and

[19] United States Department of State, *The General Pact for the
Renunciation of War, Text* (Washington, 1928), pp. 1-3.

Frank B. Kellogg, the American Secretary of State, was a comprehensive plan to abolish war "as an instrument of international policy." The Pact was accepted later by nearly all the nations of the world.

✓   ✓   ✓

The President of the German Reich, the President of the United States of America, His Majesty the King of the Belgians, the President of the French Republic, His Majesty the King of Great Britain, Ireland and the British Dominions beyond the Seas, Emperor of India, His Majesty the King of Italy, His Majesty the Emperor of Japan, the President of the Republic of Poland, the President of the Czechoslovak Republic,

Deeply sensible of their solemn duty to promote the welfare of mankind;

Persuaded that the time has come when a frank renunciation of war as an instrument of national policy should be made to the end that the peaceful and friendly relations now existing between their peoples may be perpetuated;

Convinced that all changes in their relations with one another should be sought only by pacific means and be the result of a peaceful and orderly process, and that any signatory Power which shall hereafter seek to promote its national interests by resort to war should be denied the benefits furnished by this Treaty;

Hopeful that, encouraged by their example, all the other nations of the world will join in this humane endeavor and by adhering to the present Treaty as soon as it comes into force bring their peoples within the scope of its beneficent provisions, thus uniting the civilized nations of the world in a common renunciation of war as an instrument of their national policy;

Have decided to conclude a Treaty and . . . have agreed upon the following articles:

ARTICLE 1. The High Contracting Parties solemnly declare in the names of their respective peoples that they condemn recourse to war for the solution of international controversies, and renounce it as an instrument of national policy in their relations with one another.

ARTICLE 2. The High Contracting Parties agree that the settlement or solution of all disputes or conflicts

of whatever nature or of whatever origin they may be,
which may arise among them, shall never be sought except by pacific means.

ARTICLE 3. The present Treaty shall be ratified by
the High Contracting Parties . . . in accordance with
their respective constitutional requirements. . . .

This Treaty shall . . . remain open as long as may be
necessary for adherence by all the other Powers of the
world. Every instrument evidencing the adherence of a
Power shall be deposited at Washington. . . .

It shall be the duty of the . . . United States to furnish
each Government named in the Preamble and every Government subsequently adhering to this Treaty with a certified copy of the Treaty and of every instrument of ratification or adherence.

THE ESCALATOR CLAUSE OF THE LONDON NAVAL TREATY, APRIL 22, 1930[20]

The London Naval Conference of 1930 sought not so
much to reduce naval armaments as limit them. The continuing suspicions of the signatories were betrayed by including the following "escalator clause," which permitted
each power to exceed the tonnage limits if in its opinion
new construction by any non-signatory power threatened
its own security.

[20] For the complete text see League of Nations, *Treaty Series
1931*, CXII, pp. 66-91.

ARTICLE 21. If, during the term of the present Treaty, the requirements of the national security of any High Contracting Party in respect of vessels of war limited by Part III of the present Treaty are, in the opinion of that Party, materially affected by new construction of any other Power than those who have joined in Part III of this Treaty, that High Contracting Party will notify the other Parties to Part III as to the increases required to be made in its own tonnages within one or more of the categories of such vessels of war, specifying particularly the proposed increases and the reasons therefor, and shall be entitled to make such increase. Thereupon the other Parties to Part III of this Treaty shall be entitled to make a proportionate increase in the category or categories specified; and the said other Parties shall promptly advise with each other through diplomatic channels as to the situation thus presented.

— 19 —

QUADRAGESIMO ANNO: POPE PIUS XI ON RECONSTRUCTING THE SOCIAL ORDER, MAY 15, 1931 [21]

In 1891 Pope Leo XIII, in his famous encyclical, *Rerum Novarum,* sought to stimulate a Catholic social

[21] *Quadragesimo Anno: Encyclical Letter of Pope Pius XI on Reconstructing the Social Order* (New York, 1931), pp. 19, 43, 48.

movement which, opposing economic liberalism on the
one hand and Marxian socialism on the other, would aim
at the Christianizing of modern industrial society. On
May 15, 1931, on the fortieth anniversary of Leo XIII's
encyclical, Pius XI reaffirmed and developed the principles and program of Catholic social reform as outlined
by his predecessor. Following are extracts from Pius XI's
encyclical letter, *Quadragesimo Anno*.

✓   ✓   ✓

Now the natural law, or rather, God's Will manifested
by it, demands that right order be observed in the application of natural resources to human need; and this order
consists in everything having its proper owner. Hence it
follows that unless a man apply his labor to his own property, an alliance must be formed between his toil and his
neighbor's property, for each is helpless without the other.
This was what Leo XIII had in mind when he wrote:
"Capital cannot do without labor, nor labor without capital." It is therefore entirely false to ascribe the results
of their combined efforts to either party alone; and it is
flagrantly unjust that either should deny the efficacy of
the other and seize all the profits. . . .

Economic life must be inspired by Christian principles.
For this pitiable ruin of souls, which if it continue, will
frustrate all efforts to reform society, there can be no
other remedy than a frank and sincere return to the
teaching of the Gospel. Men must observe anew the pre-
cepts of Him Who alone has the words of eternal life,
words which even though Heaven and earth be changed,
shall not pass away.

All those versed in social matters demand a rationaliza-
tion of economic life which will introduce sound and true
order. But this order, which We ourselves desire and
make every effort to promote, will necessarily be quite
faulty and imperfect, unless all man's activities harmoni-
ously unite to imitate and, as far as is humanly possible,
attain the marvelous unity of the divine plan. This is the
perfect order which the Church preaches, with intense
earnestness, and which right reason demands: which
places God as the first and supreme end of all created
activity, and regards all created goods as mere instru-

ments under God, to be used only in so far as they help towards the attainment of our supreme end.

Nor is it to be imagined that remunerative occupations are thereby belittled or deemed less consonant with human dignity. On the contrary, we are taught to recognize and reverence in them the manifest will of God the Creator, Who placed man upon earth to work it and use it in various ways to supply his needs. Those who are engaged in production are not forbidden to increase their fortunes in a lawful and just manner: indeed it is just that he who renders service to society and develops its wealth should himself have his proportionate share of the increased public riches, provided always that he respects the laws of God and the rights of his neighbor, and uses his property in accord with faith and right reason. If these principles be observed by all, everywhere and at all times, not merely the production and acquisition of goods, but also the use of wealth, now so often uncontrolled, will within a short time be brought back again to the standards of equity and just distribution. . . .

That this happy result may be attained, Venerable Brethren and Beloved Children, We impart to you all members of the great Catholic family entrusted to Our care, but with special affection of Our heart to artisans and other workingmen engaged in manual labor, by Divine Providence committed to Us in a particular manner, and to Christian employers and masters, with paternal affection the Apostolic Benediction.

Given at Rome, at Saint Peter's, the fifteenth day of May, in the year 1931, the tenth of Our pontificate.

PIUS PP. XI.

THE STATUTE OF WESTMINSTER, DECEMBER 11, 1931 [22]

The Statute of Westminster, passed by the British Parliament in December, 1931, made legal the new status of the British dominions. The last vestiges of the old British Empire were wiped out by the formation of the British Commonwealth of Independent Nations. Following are the key paragraphs of the Statute.

✓   ✓   ✓

. . . Whereas . . . inasmuch as the Crown is the symbol of the free association of the members of the British Commonwealth of Nations, and as they are united by a common allegiance to the Crown, it would be in accord with the established constitutional position of all the members of the Commonwealth in relation to one another that any alteration in the law touching the Succession to the Throne or the Royal Style and Titles shall hereafter require the assent as well of the Parliaments of the Dominions as of the Parliaments of the United Kingdom;

And whereas it is in accord with the established constitutional position that no law hereafter made by the Parliament of the United Kingdom shall extend to any of the said Dominions as part of the law of that Dominion otherwise than at the request and with the consent of that Dominion;

And whereas the Dominion of Canada, the Commonwealth of Australia, the Dominion of New Zealand, the Union of South Africa, the Irish Free State, and Newfoundland have severally requested and consented to the submission of a measure to the Parliament of the United Kingdom for making such provision with regard to the matters aforesaid as is hereafter in this Act contained:

[22] *The Public General Acts of Great Britain*, 1932 (London, 1933), pp. 13-17, *passim.*

Now, therefore, be it enacted by the King's most Excellent Majesty by and with the consent of the Lord Spiritual and Temporal, and Commons, in this present Parliament assembled, and by the authority of the same, as follows: . . .

2. a. The Colonial Laws Validity Act, 1865, shall not apply to any law made after the commencement of this Act by the Parliament of a Dominion.

b. No law and no provision of any law made after the commencement of this Act by the Parliament of a Dominion shall be void or inoperative on the ground that it is repugnant to the law of England. . . .

3. It is hereby declared and enacted that the Parliament of a Dominion has full power to make laws having extra-territorial operation.

4. No Act of Parliament of the United Kingdom passed after the commencement of this Act shall extend or be deemed to extend, to a Dominion as part of the law of that Dominion, unless it is expressly declared in that Act that that Dominion has requested, and consented to, the enactment thereof. . . .

— 21 —

THE NUREMBERG LAWS ON CITIZENSHIP AND RACE, SEPTEMBER-NOVEMBER, 1935 [23]

The most spectacular and immediate consequence of the Nazi triumph was the reign of anti-Semitism. From

[23] *Reichgesetzblatt,* 1935, No. 100, September 15, 1935, I: 1142-47.

September to November 1935 Hitler introduced the so-called Nuremberg, or Ghetto Laws, which placed anti-Semitism in the category of legal legislation. This was the first time in history that prejudice and intolerance were deliberately incorporated into the laws of a great nation.

✔   ✔   ✔

I. The Reich Citizenship Law of September 15, 1935

The Reichstag has adopted by unanimous vote the following law which is herewith promulgated.

ARTICLE 1. (1) A subject of the State is one who belongs to the protective union of the German Reich, and who, therefore, has specific obligations to the Reich.

(2) The status of subject is to be acquired in accordance with the provisions of the Reich and the State Law of Citizenship.

ARTICLE 2. (1) A citizen of the Reich may be only that subject who is of German or kindred blood, and who, through his behavior, shows that he is both desirous and personally fit to serve loyally the German people and the Reich.

(2) The right to citizenship is obtained by the granting of Reich citizenship papers.

(3) Only the citizen of the Reich may enjoy full political rights in consonance with the provisions of the laws.

ARTICLE 3. The Reich Minister of the Interior, in conjunction with the Deputy to the *Fuehrer* will issue the required legal and administrative decrees for the implementation and amplification of this law.

Promulgated: September 16, 1935.

In force: September 30, 1935

I a. First Supplementary Decree of November 14, 1935

On the basis of Article 3 of the Reich Law of Citizenship of September 15, 1935, the following is hereby decreed:

ARTICLE 1. (1) Until further provisions concerning citizenship papers, all subjects of German or kindred blood who possessed the right to vote in the Reichstag elections when the Law of Citizenship came into effect, shall, for the present, possess the rights of Reich citizens. The same shall be true of those upon whom the Reich Minister of the Interior, in conjunction with the Deputy to the *Fuehrer,* shall confer citizenship.

(2) The Reich Minister of the Interior, in conjunction with the Deputy to the *Fuehrer,* may revoke citizenship.

ARTICLE 2. (1) The provisions of Article 1 shall apply also to subjects who are of mixed Jewish blood.

(2) An individual of mixed Jewish blood is one who is descended from one or two grandparents who, racially, were full Jews, in so far that he is not a Jew according to Section 2 of Article 5. Full-blooded Jewish grandparents are those who belonged to the Jewish religious community.

ARTICLE 3. Only citizens of the Reich, as bearers of full political rights, can exercise the right of voting in political matters, and have the right to hold public office. The Reich Minister of the Interior, or any agency he empowers, can make exceptions during the transition period on the matter of holding public office. These measures do not apply to matters concerning religious organizations.

ARTICLE 4. (1) A Jew cannot be a citizen of the Reich. He cannot exercise the right to vote; he cannot occupy public office.

(2) Jewish officials will be retired as of December 31, 1935. In the event that such officials served at the front in the World War either for Germany or her allies, they shall receive as pension, until they reach the age limit, the full salary last received, on the basis of which their pension would have been computed. They shall not, however, be promoted according to their seniority in rank. When they reach the age limit, their pension will be computed again, according to the salary last received on which their pension was to be calculated.

(3) These provisions do not concern the affairs of religious organizations.

(4) The conditions regarding service of teachers in public Jewish schools will remain unchanged until the promulgation of new regulations on the Jewish school system.

ARTICLE 5. (1) A Jew is an individual who is descended from at least three grandparents who were, racially, full Jews. . . .

(2) A Jew is also an individual who is descended from two full-Jewish grandparents if:

(a) he was a member of the Jewish religious community when this law was issued, or who joined the community later;

(b) when the law was issued he was married to a person who was a Jew, or was subsequently married to a Jew;

(c) he is the issue from a marriage with a Jew, in the sense of Section 1, which was contracted after the coming into effect of the Law for the Protection of German Blood and Honor of September 15, 1935;

(d) he is the issue of an extra-marital relationship with a Jew, according to Section I, and will have been born out of wedlock after July 31, 1936.

ARTICLE 6. (1) In so far as there are, in the laws of the Reich or in the decrees of the National Socialist Labor Party and its affiliates, certain requirements for the purity of German blood which extend beyond Article 5, the same remain untouched.

(2) Other requirements for the purity of the blood that go beyond Article 5 may be submitted only with the consent of the Minister of the Interior and the Deputy to the *Fuehrer*. Any such requirements already in existence shall be discarded after January 1, 1936, unless they have been permitted by the Minister of the Interior, in conjunction with the Deputy to the *Fuehrer*. All proposals for admission must be presented to the Reich Minister of the Interior.

ARTICLE 7. The *Fuehrer* and Chancellor of the Reich is empowered to release anyone from the provisions of these administrative decrees.

II. The Law for the Protection of German Blood and Honor, September 15, 1935

Imbued with the knowledge that the purity of German blood is the necessary prerequisite for the existence of the German nation, and inspired by an inflexible will to maintain the existence of the German nation for all future times, the Reichstag has unanimously adopted the following law, which is now proclaimed:

ARTICLE 1. (1) Any marriages between Jews and citizens of German or kindred blood are herewith forbidden. Marriages entered into despite this law are invalid, even if they are arranged abroad as a means of circumventing this law.

(2) Annulment proceedings for marriages may be initiated only by the Public Prosecutor.

ARTICLE 2. Extramarital relations between Jews and citizens of German or kindred blood are herewith forbidden.

ARTICLE 3. Jews are forbidden to employ as servants in their households female subjects of German or kindred blood who are under the age of 45 years.

ARTICLE 4. (1) Jews are prohibited from displaying the Reich and national flag and from showing the national colors.

(2) However, they may display the Jewish colors. The exercise of this right is under State protection.

ARTICLE 5. (1) Anyone who acts contrary to the prohibition noted in Article 1 renders himself liable to penal servitude.

(2) The man who acts contrary to the prohibition of Article 2 will be punished by sentence to either a jail or penitentiary.

(3) Anyone who acts contrary to the provisions of Articles 3 and 4 will be punished with a jail sentence up to a year and with a fine, or with either of these penalties.

ARTICLE 6. The Reich Minister of Interior, in conjunction with the Deputy to the *Fuehrer* and the Reich Minister of Justice, will issue the required legal and administrative decrees for the implementation and amplification of this law.

ARTICLE 7. This law shall go into effect on the day following its promulgation, with the exception of Article 3, which shall go into effect on January 1, 1936.

OPENING CHAPTER OF THE SOVIET CONSTITUTION OF DECEMBER 5, 1936[24]

The Soviet Constitution of 1936, often called "Stalin's Constitution," was adopted by the All-Union Congress of Soviets and proclaimed to be the most democratic constitution of the world. On paper, but on paper alone, there is much to support this claim of "democracy." Following is the opening chapter of the constitution.

✔   ✔   ✔

CHAPTER I

THE ORGANIZATION OF SOCIETY

ARTICLE 1. The Union of Soviet Socialist Republics is a socialist State of workers and peasants.

ARTICLE 2. The political basis of the U.S.S.R. is formed by the councils (soviets) of toilers' deputies, which have developed and become strong as a result of the overthrow of the power of the landlords and capitalists and the winning of the dictatorship of the proletariat.

ARTICLE 3. All power in the U.S.S.R. belongs to the toilers of city and village as represented by the councils of toilers' deputies.

ARTICLE 4. The economic basis of the U.S.S.R. is formed by the socialist system of economy and the socialist ownership of implements and means of production, which have been firmly established as a result of the liquidation of the capitalistic system of economy, the abolition of private ownership of implements and means of production, and the destruction of the exploitation of man by man.

[24] Carnegie Endowment for International Peace, *International Conciliation*, No. 327 (1937), pp. 143 ff. Translated by C. A. Manning.

ARTICLE 5. Socialist ownership in the U.S.S.R. has either the form of State ownership (the property of the whole people), or the form of cooperative-collective ownership (the property of individual collective farms, the property of cooperative associations).

ARTICLE 6. The land, its deposits, waters, forests, mills, factories, shafts, mines, railroad, water and air transport, banks, means of communication, large agricultural undertakings organized by the State and also communal undertakings and the fundamental fund of dwellings in cities and industrial points, are State property, that is the property of the whole people.

ARTICLE 7. Public undertakings in the collective farms and cooperative organizations with their livestock and implements, production effected by the collective farms and cooperative organizations, as well as their public structures are the public, social property of the collective farms and cooperative organizations.

Each collective farm household, aside from its basic income from the public collective farm economy, has for its own use a small piece of land attached to the homestead and as individual property the auxiliary economy on this attached piece, a dwelling house, productive livestock, poultry and minor agricultural implements—in accordance with the regulation of the agricultural artel.

ARTICLE 8. The land occupied by collective farms is secured to them for use without payment and without time limit, that is, forever.

ARTICLE 9. Along with the socialist system of economy, which is the prevailing form of economy in the U.S.S.R., there is permitted by law small private economy of individual peasants and handicraftsmen, based on their personal labor and excluding the exploitation of the labor of another person.

ARTICLE 10. The right of personal property of citizens in the income from their toil and in their savings, in their dwelling house and auxiliary domestic economy, in articles of their domestic economy and use, in articles of personal use and comfort, as well as the right of inheritance of personal property of citizens—are protected by law.

ARTICLE 11. The economic life of the U.S.S.R. is defined and directed by the State plan of national economy in the interests of the increase of the public wealth, the constant rising of the material and cultural level of the toilers, the strengthening of the independence of the U.S.S.R., and the strengthening of its defensive ability.

ARTICLE 12. Toil in the U.S.S.R. is an obligation and a matter of honor of each citizen who is fit for toil, according to the principle: "He who does not work does not eat."

In the U.S.S.R. there is being realized the principle of socialism: "From each according to his ability, to each according to his toil."

— 23 —

ABDICATION LETTER OF EDWARD VIII TO THE HOUSE OF COMMONS, DECEMBER 10, 1936[25]

On January 20, 1936, King George V, who had ruled Great Britain since 1910, died at the age of seventy. His successor, Edward VIII, abdicated in less than a year, when the Prime Minister, Stanley Baldwin, and the Church of England opposed the new king's desire to marry an American who had been twice divorced.

[25] Great Britain, *Parliamentary Debates, House of Commons,* Vol. 318, pp. 2175-76.

Fort Belvedere
Sunningdale
Berkshire

Members of the House of Commons,

After long and anxious consideration, I have determined to renounce the Throne to which I succeeded on the death of My father, and I am now communicating this, My final and irrevocable decision. Realising as I do the gravity of this step, I can only hope that I shall have the understanding of My peoples in the decision I have taken and the reasons which have led Me to take it. I will not enter now into My private feelings, but I would beg that it should be remembered that the burden which constantly rests upon the shoulders of a Sovereign is so heavy that it can only be borne in circumstances different from those in which I now find Myself. I conceive that I am not overlooking the duty that rests on Me to place in the forefront the public interest, when I declare that I am conscious that I can no longer discharge this heavy task with efficiency or with satisfaction to Myself.

I have accordingly this morning executed an Instrument of Abdication in the terms following:—

"I, Edward VIII, of Great Britain, Ireland, and the British Dominions beyond the Seas, King, Emperor of India, do hereby declare My irrevocable determination to renounce the Throne for Myself and for my descendants, and My desire that effect should be given to this Instrument of Abdication immediately.

In token whereof I have hereunto set My hand this tenth day of December, nineteen hundred and thirty-six, in the presence of the witnesses whose signatures are subscribed.

EDWARD R.I.

My execution of this Instrument has been witnessed by My three brothers, Their Royal Highnesses the Duke of York, the Duke of Gloucester and the Duke of Kent.

I deeply appreciate the spirit which has actuated the appeals which have been made to Me to take a different decision, and I have, before reaching My final determination, most fully pondered over them. But My mind is made up. Moreover, further delay cannot but be most

80

injurious to the peoples whom I have tried to serve as
Prince of Wales and as King and whose future happiness
and prosperity are the constant wish of My heart.

I take My leave of them in the confident hope that the
course which I have thought it right to follow is that
which is best for the stability of the Throne and Empire
and the happiness of My peoples. I am deeply sensible
of the consideration which they have always extended
to Me both before and after My accession to the Throne
and which I know they will extend in full measure to My
successor.

I am most anxious that there should be no delay of any
kind in giving effect to the Instrument which I have
executed and that all necessary steps should be taken
immediately to secure that My lawful successor, My
brother, His Royal Highness, the Duke of York, should
ascend the Throne.

EDWARD R.I.

— 24 —

THE HOSSBACH DOCUMENT, NOVEMBER 5, 1937[26]

At a secret meeting held on November 5, 1937, Hitler
outlined to his military leaders the practical steps in
undertaking aggression against other countries. The
minutes of the meeting, as recorded by Hitler's adjutant,

[26] From *Proceedings of the International Military Tribunal,
Trial of the Major War Criminals* (Nuremberg, 1947-49),
as quoted in G. M. Gilbert, *Psychology of Dictatorship*
(New York, 1950), pp. 99-100.

Colonel Hossbach, reveal how Hitler planned to wage war
two years before the outbreak of hostilities.

✓   ✓   ✓

The *Fuehrer* then stated: The aim of German policy is
the security and the preservation of the *Volk* and its
propagation. This is consequently a problem of space. . . .
The question for Germany is where the greatest possible
conquest can be made at lowest cost.

German politics must reckon with its two hateful enemies, England and France, to whom a strong German
colossus in the center of Europe would be intolerable.
Both these states would oppose a further reinforcement of
Germany, both in Europe and overseas, and in this opposition they would have the support of all parties. . . .

If the *Fuehrer* is still living, then it will be his irrevocable decision to solve the German space problem no later
than 1943-45. . . . For the improvement of our military
political position it must be our first aim, in every case
of entanglement by war, to conquer Czechoslovakia and
Austria simultaneously, in order to remove any threat
from the flanks in case of a possible advance west-
ward. . . . Once Czechoslovakia is conquered—and a
mutual frontier of Germany-Hungary is obtained—then a
neutral attitude by Poland in a German-French conflict
could be more easily relied upon. Our agreements with
Poland remain valid only as long as Germany's strength
remains unshakeable. . . .

The *Fuehrer* believes personally, that in all probability
England and perhaps also France, have already silently
written off Czechoslovakia. . . . Without England's support it would also not be necessary to take into consideration a march by France through Holland and Belgium. . . . Naturally, we should in every case have to
secure our frontier during the operation of our attacks
against Czechoslovakia and Austria. . . .

Military preparation by Russia must be countered by
the speed of our operations; it is a question whether this
needs to be taken into consideration at all, in view of
Japan's attitude. . . .

Feldmarschall von Blomberg and Generaloberst von
Fritsch, in giving their estimate of the situation, repeat-

edly pointed out that we should not run the risk that England and France become our enemies. . . .

In view of the information given by the *Fuehrer,* Generaloberst Goering considered it imperative to think of a reduction of our military undertaking in Spain. . . .

— 25 —

THE MUNICH AGREEMENT, SEPTEMBER 29, 1938[27]

After annexing Austria on March 12, 1938, Hitler demanded that the Sudeten Germans of Czechoslovakia be placed under German rule. Believing that Europe was rushing headlong into war, the British Prime Minister, Neville Chamberlain, called for a conference. On September 29, Chamberlain, Daladier, Hitler, and Mussolini concluded the Munich Agreement. Czechoslovakia was sold down the river in a classic move of appeasement.

Germany, the United Kingdom, France, and Italy, taking into consideration the agreement, which has been already reached in principle for the cession to Germany of the Sudeten German territory, have agreed on the following terms and conditions. . . .

1. The evacuation will begin on October 1st.
2. The United Kingdom, France, and Italy agree that the evacuation of the territory shall be completed by

[27] Great Britain, *Parliamentary Papers,* 1937-38, XXX, Miscellaneous No. 8 (1938), Cmd. 5848, 3-5.

October 10th, without any existing installations having been destroyed, and that the Czechoslovak Government will be held responsible for carrying out the evacuation without damage to the said installations.

3. The conditions governing the evacuation will be laid down in detail by an international Commission composed of representatives of Germany, the United Kingdom, France, Italy, and Czechoslovakia.

4. The occupation by stages of the predominantly German territory by German troops will begin on the 1st October. . . .

5. The international Commission referred to in paragraph 3 will determine the territories in which a plebiscite is to be held. . . .

6. The final determination of the frontiers will be carried out by the international Commission. . . .

7. There will be a right of option into and out of the transferred territories . . . to be exercised within six months. . . .

8. The Czechoslovak Government will within a period of four weeks . . . release from their military and police forces any Sudeten Germans who may wish to be released. . . .

Annex to the Agreement: His Majesty's Government in the United Kingdom and the French Government have entered into the above agreement on the basis that they stand by the offer . . . relating to an international guarantee of the new boundaries of the Czechoslovak State against unprovoked aggression. . . .

Declaration. The Heads of the Governments of the four Powers declare that the problems of the Polish and Hungarian minorities in Czechoslovakia, if not settled within three months by agreement between the respective Governments, shall form the subject of another meeting of the Heads of the Governments of the four Powers here present.

Munich, September 29, 1938

> Adolf Hitler
> Neville Chamberlain
> Edouard Daladier
> Benito Mussolini

26

WINSTON CHURCHILL'S THREE FAMOUS SPEECHES OF 1940

British morale in World War II was strongly stimulated by three extraordinary speeches made by Prime Minister Winston S. Churchill. The significant portions of these addresses, which received worldwide attention, are reproduced below.

A

"Blood, Toil, Tears and Sweat," May 13, 1940 [28]

In his first speech as Prime Minister, Churchill addressed the House of Commons on the Battle of Britain in words that have since become famous.

✔   ✔   ✔

. . . In this crisis I hope I may be pardoned if I do not address the House at any length today. I hope that any of my friends and colleagues, or former colleagues, who are affected by the political reconstruction, will make allowance, all allowance, for any lack of ceremony with which it has been necessary to act. I would say to the House, as I said to those who have joined this Government; "I have nothing to offer but blood, toil, tears and sweat."

We have before us an ordeal of the most grievous kind. We have before us many, many long months of struggle and of suffering. You ask, what is our policy? I will say: It is to wage war, by sea, land, and air, with all our might and with all the strength that God can give us: to wage war against a monstrous tyranny, never surpassed in the dark, lamentable catalogue of human crime. That is our policy. You ask, what is our aim? I can answer in one word: It is victory, victory at all costs, victory in spite of all terror, victory, however long and

[28] Great Britain, *Parliamentary Debates, House of Commons,* 5th Series, CCCLX, p. 1502.

hard the road may be; for without victory there is no survival. Let that be realized; no survival for the British Empire; no survival for all that the British Empire has stood for, no survival for the urge and impulse of the ages, that mankind will move forward towards its goal. But I take up my task with buoyancy and hope. I feel sure that our cause will not be suffered to fail among men. At this time I feel entitled to claim the aid of all, and I say, "Come, then, let us go forward together with our united strength."

B
"Their Finest Hour," June 18, 1940 [29]

The collapse of France moved Churchill to another great speech, delivered before the House of Commons on June 18, 1940, in which he linked the coming Battle of Britain with the survival of Christian civilization.

✦   ✦   ✦

. . . What General Weygand called the "Battle of France" is over. I expect that the battle of Britain is about to begin. Upon this battle depends the survival of Christian civilization. Upon it depends our own British life and the long continuity of our institutions and our Empire. The whole fury and might of the enemy must very soon be turned on us. Hitler knows that he will have to break us in this island or lose the war. If we can stand up to him all Europe may be free and the life of the world may move forward into broad, sunlit uplands; but if we fail then the whole world, including the United States, and all that we have known and cared for, will sink into the abyss of a new dark age made more sinister, and perhaps more prolonged, by the lights of a perverted science. Let us, therefore, brace ourselves to our duty and so bear ourselves that if the British Commonwealth and Empire lasts for a thousand years men will still say, "This was their finest hour."

[29] Great Britain, *Parliamentary Debates, House of Commons,* 5th Series, CCCLXII, pp. 60-61.

C

"So Much Owed by so Many to so Few," August 20, 1940 [30]

Churchill's tribute to the Royal Air Force was made in a speech to the House of Commons on August 20, 1940. A master of English prose, Churchill was awarded the 1953 Nobel Prize for Literature.

✓   ✓   ✓

. . . The gratitude of every home in our Island, in our Empire, and indeed throughout the world, except in the abodes of the guilty, goes out to the British airmen who, undaunted by odds, unwearied in their constant challenge and mortal danger, are turning the tide of world war by their prowess and by their devotion. Never in the field of human conflict was so much owed by so many to so few. All hearts go out to the fighter pilots, whose brilliant actions we see with our own eyes day after day, but we must never forget that all the time, night after night, month after month, our bomber squadrons travel far into Germany, find their targets in the darkness by the highest navigational skill, aim their attacks, often under the heaviest fire, often with serious loss, with deliberate, careful discrimination, and inflict shattering blows upon the whole of the technical and war-making structure of the Nazi power. . . .

[30] Great Britain, *Parliamentary Debates, House of Commons,* 5th Series, CCCLXIV, pp. 1166-67.

27

THE ROME-BERLIN-TOKYO AXIS PACT, SEPTEMBER 27, 1940[31]

On September 27, 1940, Germany, Italy, and Japan signed a Tripartite Pact agreeing to assist each other in case another power became involved in the war in Europe or in the Far East.

✓   ✓   ✓

The Governments of Germany, Italy, and Japan consider it the prerequisite of lasting peace that every nation in the world shall receive the space to which it is entitled. They have, therefore, decided to stand by and co-operate with one another in their efforts in Greater East Asia and the regions of Europe respectively. In doing this it is their prime purpose to establish and maintain a new order of things, calculated to promote the mutual prosperity and welfare of the peoples concerned.

It is, furthermore, the desire of the three Governments to extend co-operation to other nations . . . who are inclined to direct their efforts along lines similar to their own for the purpose of realizing their ultimate object, world peace.

Accordingly, the Governments of Germany, Italy and Japan have agreed as follows:

ARTICLE 1. Japan recognizes and respects the leadership of Germany and Italy in the establishment of a new order in Europe.

ARTICLE 2. Germany and Italy recognize and respect the leadership of Japan in the establishment of a new order in Greater East Asia.

ARTICLE 3. Germany, Italy and Japan agree to co-operate in their efforts on the aforesaid lines. They further undertake to assist one another with all political,

[31] German Library of Information, *Facts in Review* (New York, 1941), II, p. 486.

economic and military means if one of the three Contracting Powers is attacked by a Power at present not involved
in the European War or in the Chinese-Japanese conflict

ARTICLE 4. With a view to implementing the present pact, joint technical commissions, the members of
which are to be appointed by the governments of Germany, Italy, and Japan, will meet without delay.

ARTICLE 6. The present pact shall become valid immediately upon signature and shall remain in force ten
years. . . .

Done in triplicate at Berlin, the 27th day of September,
1940, in the eighteenth year of the Fascist era, correspond-
ing to the 27th day of the ninth month of the fifteenth
year of Showa.

— 28 —

PRESIDENT FRANKLIN D. ROOSE-
VELT'S FOUR FREEDOMS SPEECH,
JANUARY 6, 1941 [32]

In his address to Congress on Jaunary 6, 1941, and
reaffirmed in his address of January 6, 1942, President
Franklin D. Roosevelt enunciated the famous "Four
Freedoms," which he presented as a contribution to the
discussion of American peace aims. Here is the conclud-
ing section of the speech.

✦   ✦   ✦

In the future days, which we seek to make secure, we
look forward to a world founded upon four essential
human freedoms.

[32] *Congressional Record*, LXXXVII (January 6, 1941), p. 46.

The first is freedom of speech and expression, everywhere in the world.

The second is freedom of every person to worship God in his own way—everywhere in the world.

The third is freedom from want—which, translated into world terms, means economic understandings which will secure to every nation a healthy peacetime life for its inhabitants—everywhere in the world.

The fourth is freedom from fear—which, translated into world terms, means a world-wide reduction of armaments to such a point and in such a thorough fashion that no nation will be in a position to commit an act of physical aggression against any neighbor—anywhere in the world.

That is no vision of a distant millennium. It is a definite basis for a kind of world attainable in our own time and generation. That kind of world is the very antithesis of the so-called new order of tyranny which the dictators seek to create with the crash of a bomb.

To that new order we oppose the greater conception—the moral order. A good society is able to face schemes of world domination and foreign revolutions alike without fear.

Since the beginning of our American history, we have been engaged in change—in a perpetual peaceful revolution—a revolution which goes on steadily, quietly adjusting itself to changing conditions—without the concentration camp or the quick-lime in the ditch. The world order which we seek is the cooperation of free countries, working together in a friendly, civilized society.

This nation has placed its destiny in the hands and hearts of its millions of free men and women; and its faith in freedom under the guidance of God. Freedom means the supremacy of human rights everywhere. Our support goes to those who struggle to gain those rights or keep them. Our strength is our unity of purpose.

To that high concept there can be no end save victory.

— 29 —

THE ATLANTIC CHARTER, AUGUST 14, 1941 [33]

President Rooesvelt and Prime Minister Churchill met off the coast of Newfoundland in August, 1941, in the first of their wartime conferences. The outcome of this conference, the Atlantic Charter, was a general statement of policy in which the two leaders pledged allegiance to democratic principles and promised to work for a world in which political and economic equality would prevail among nations "after the final destruction of the Nazi tyranny."

✶   ✶   ✶

The President of the United States and the Prime Minister, Mr. Churchill, representing His Majesty's Government in the United Kingdom, have met at sea.

They have been accompanied by officials of their two governments, including high ranking officers of their military, naval and air services.

The whole problem of the supply of munitions of war, as provided by the Lease-Lend Act, for the armed forces of the United States and for those countries actively engaged in resisting aggression has been further examined.

Lord Beaverbrook, the Minister of Supply of the British Government, has joined in these conferences. He is going to proceed to Washington to discuss further details with appropriate officials of the United States Government. These conferences will also cover the supply problems of the Soviet Union.

The President and the Prime Minister have had several conferences. They have considered the dangers to world

[33] Congressional Record, LXXXVII (77th Congress, 1st Session), p. 7217.

civilization arising from the policies of military domination by conquest upon which the Hitlerite government of Germany and other governments associated therewith have embarked, and have made clear the steps which their countries are respectively taking for their safety in the face of these dangers.

They have agreed upon the following joint declaration:

The President of the United States of American and the Prime Minister, Mr. Churchill, representing His Majesty's Government in the United Kingdom, being met together, deem it right to make known certain common principles in the national policies of their respective countries on which they base their hopes for a better future for the world.

First, their countries seek no aggrandizement, territorial or other;

Second, they desire to see no territorial changes that do not accord with the freely expressed wishes of the peoples concerned;

Third, they respect the right of all peoples to choose the form of government under which they will live; and they wish to see sovereign rights and self-government restored to those who have been forcibly deprived of them;

Fourth, they will endeavor, with due respect for their existing obligations, to further the enjoyment by all States, great or small, victor or vanquished, of access, on equal terms, to the trade and to the raw materials of the world which are needed for their economic prosperity;

Fifth, they desire to bring about the fullest collaboration between all nations in the economic field with the object of securing, for all, improved labor standards, economic adjustment and social security;

Sixth, after the final destruction of the Nazi tyranny, they hope to see established a peace which will afford all nations the means of dwelling in safety within their own boundaries, and which will afford assurance that all the men in all the lands may live out their lives in freedom from fear and want;

Seventh, such a peace should enable all men to traverse the high seas and oceans without hindrance;

Eighth, they believe that all of the nations of the world, for realistic as well as spiritual reasons, must come to the abandonment of the use of force. Since no future peace can be maintained if land, sea or air armaments continue to be employed by nations which threaten, or may threaten, aggression outside of their frontiers, they believe, pending the establishment of a wider and permanent system of general security, that the disarmament of such nations is essential. They will likewise aid and encourage all other practicable measures which will lighten for peace-loving peoples the crushing burden of armaments.

FRANKLIN D. ROOSEVELT
WINSTON S. CHURCHILL

— 30 —

WAR MESSAGE OF PRESIDENT ROOSEVELT ON JAPAN, DECEMBER 8, 1941 [34]

When Japan attacked American possessions in the Pacific on December 7, 1941, she effectively wiped out any internal dissension that existed in the United States. The next day, December 8, President Roosevelt read his famous war message to Congress. The Senate passed a formal declaration of war unanimously, while the House passed it with only one dissenting vote.

✱   ✱   ✱

Yesterday, December 7, 1941—A date which will live in infamy—the United States of America was suddenly

[34] Text in *World Almanac*, 1942.

and deliberately attacked by naval and air forces of the Empire of Japan.

The United States was at peace with that nation and, at the solicitation of Japan, was still in conversation with its Government and its Emperor looking toward the maintenance of peace in the Pacific.

Indeed, one hour after Japanese air squadrons had commenced bombing Oahu, the Japanese Ambassador to the United States and his colleague delivered to the Secretary of State a formal reply to a recent American message. While this reply stated that it seemed useless to continue the existing diplomatic negotiations, it contained no threat or hint of war or armed attack.

It will be recorded that the distance of Hawaii from Japan makes it obvious that the attack was deliberately planned many days or even weeks ago. During the intervening time, the Japanese Government has deliberately sought to deceive the United States by false statements and expressions of hope for continued peace.

The attack yesterday on the Hawaiian Islands has caused severe damage to American naval and military forces. Very many American lives have been lost. In addition, American ships have been reported torpedoed on the high seas between San Francisco and Honolulu.

Yesterday the Japanese Government also launched an attack against Malaya.

Last night Japanese forces attacked Hong Kong.

Last night Japanese forces attacked Guam.

Last night Japanese forces attacked the Philippine Islands.

Last night the Japanese attacked Wake Island.

This morning the Japanese attacked Midway Island.

Japan has, therefore, undertaken a surprise offensive extending throughout the Pacific area. The facts of yesterday speak for themselves. The people of the United States have already formed their opinions and well understand the implications to the very life and safety of our nation.

As Commander in Chief of the army and navy I have directed that all measures be taken for our defense.

Always will we remember the character of the onslaught against us.

No matter how long it may take us to overcome this premeditated invasion, the American people in their righteous might will win through the absolute victory.

I believe I interpret the will of the Congress and of the people when I assert that we will not only defend ourselves to the uttermost but will make very certain that this form of treachery shall never endanger us again.

Hostilities exist. There is no blinking at the fact that our people, our territory and our interests are in grave danger.

With confidence in our armed forces—with the unbounding determination of our people—we will gain the inevitable triumph—so help us God.

I ask that the Congress declare that since the unprovoked and dastardly attack by Japan on Sunday, December 7, a state of war has existed between the United States and the Japanese Empire.

FRANKLIN D. ROOSEVELT

— 31 —

DECLARATION BY THE UNITED NATIONS, JANUARY 1, 1942 [35]

On New Years Day, 1942, twenty-six nations signed a United Nations Declaration agreeing to employ all their military and economic forces to defeat the Axis and prom-

[35] United States Department of State Publication 1732, *United States Executive Agreement Series,* No. 236 (Washington, 1942).

ising that none would sign a separate peace. The idea of
a United Nations was taking hold.

↗   ↗   ↗

A joint declaration by the United States of America,
the United Kingdom of Great Britain and Northern
Ireland, the Union of Soviet Socialist Republics, China,
Australia, Belgium, Canada, Costa Rica, Cuba, Czecho-
slovakia, Dominican Republic, El Salvador, Greece, Gua-
temala, Haiti, Honduras, India, Luxembourg, Netherlands,
New Zealand, Nicaragua, Norway, Panama, Poland,
South Africa, Yugoslavia.

The Governments signatory hereto,

Having subscribed to a common program of purposes
and principles embodied in the Joint Declaration of the
President of the United States of America and the Prime
Minister of the United Kingdom of Great Britain and
Northern Ireland dated August 14, 1941, known as the
Atlantic Charter.

Being convinced that complete victory over their enemies is essential to defend life, liberty, independence and
religious freedom, and to preserve human rights and justice in their own lands as well as in other lands, and that
they are now engaged in a common struggle against sav-
age and brutal forces seeking to subjugate the world,
DECLARE:

(1) Each Government pledges itself to employ its full
resources, military or economic, against those members of
the Tripartite Pact and its adherents with which such
government is at war.

(2) Each Government pledges itself to cooperate with
the Governments signatory hereto and not to make a
separate armistice or peace with the enemies.

The foregoing declaration may be adhered to by other
nations which are, or which may be, rendering material
assistance and contributions in the struggle for victory
over Hitlerism.

Done at Washington
January First, 1942

THE CASABLANCA CONFERENCE, JANUARY 26, 1943 [36]

Meeting at Casablanca, in North Africa, in January, 1943, President Roosevelt and Prime Minister Churchill announced that the objective of the war was to obtain the unconditional surrender of Germany, Italy, and Japan.

For ten days the combined staffs have been in constant session, meeting two or three times a day, and recording progress at intervals to the President and Prime Minister.

The entire field of the war was surveyed, theater by theater, throughout the world, and all resources were marshaled for a more intense prosecution of the war by sea, land and air.

Nothing like this prolonged discussion between two Allies has ever taken place before. Complete agreement was reached between the leaders of the two countries and their respective staffs upon the war plans and enterprises to be undertaken during the campaigns of 1943 against Germany, Italy and Japan with a view to drawing the utmost advantage from the markedly favorable turn of events at the close of 1942.

Premier Stalin was cordially invited to meet the President and Prime Minister, in which case the meeting would have been held very much farther to the east. He was unable to leave Russia at this time on account of the great offensive which he himself as commander in chief is directing.

The President and the Prime Minister realized to the full the enormous weight of the war which Russia is successfully bearing along her whole land front, and their

---

[36] Text of the official communiqué from Casablanca.

prime object has been to draw as much weight as possible off the Russian armies by engaging the enemy as heavily as possible at the best selected fronts.

Premier Stalin has been fully informed of the military proposals.

The President and Prime Minister have been in communication with Generalissimo Chiang Kai-shek. They have apprised him of the measures which they are undertaking to assist him in China's magnificent and unrelaxing struggle for the common cause.

The occasion of the meeting between the President and Prime Minister made it opportune to invite General Giraud (General Henri Giraud, High Commissioner of French Africa) to confer with the combined chiefs of staff, and to arrange a meeting between him and General de Gaulle (General Charles de Gaulle, Fighting French commander). The two generals have been in close consultation.

The President and Prime Minister and their combined staffs, having completed their plans for the offensive campaigns of 1943, have now separated in order to put them into active and concerted execution.

— 33 —

THE FIRST QUEBEC CONFERENCE, AUGUST 11-24, 1943 [37]

At a meeting between President Roosevelt and Prime Minister Churchill in Washington in May 1943, a cross-

[37] Joint statement by the President of the United States and the Prime Minister of Great Britain.

channel invasion of the continent was agreed upon. This plan was further developed when the two war leaders and their staffs met at the First Quebec Conference on August 11-24, 1943.

↗   ↗   ↗

The Anglo-American War Conference which opened at Quebec on August 11 under the hospitable auspices of the Canadian Government has now concluded its work.

The whole field of world operations has been surveyed in the light of the many gratifying events which have taken place since the meeting of the President and the Prime Minister in Washington at the end of May and the necessary decisions have been taken to provide for the forward actions of the Fleets, Armies and Air Forces of the two nations.

Considering that these forces are intermingled in continuous action against the enemy in several quarters of the globe, it is indispensable that entire unity of aim and method should be maintained at the summit of the war direction.

Further conferences will be needed probably at shorter intervals than before, as the war effort of the United States and the British Commonwealth and Empire against the enemy spreads and deepens.

It would not be helpful to the fighting troops to make any announcements of the decisions which have been reached. These can only emerge in action.

It may, however, be stated that the military discussions of the Chiefs of Staff turned very largely upon the war against Japan and the bringing of effective aid to China. Mr. T. V. Soong, representing the Generalissimo Chiang Kai-shek, was a party to the discussions. In this field, as in the European, the President and the Prime Minister were able to receive and approve the unanimous recommendations of the Combined Chiefs of Staff. Agreement was also reached upon the political issues underlying or arising out of the military operations.

It was resolved to hold another conference before the end of the year between the British and American authorities, in addition to any tripartite meeting which it may be possible to arrange with Soviet Russia. Full reports of the decisions so far as they affect the war against Germany and Italy will be furnished to the Soviet Government.

Consideration has been given during the conference to the question of relations with the French Committee of Liberation, and it is understood that an announcement by a number of Governments will be made in the latter part of the week.

— 34 —

THE MOSCOW PACT DECLARATION ON GENERAL SECURITY, OCTOBER 30, 1943 [38]

On October 30, 1943, the chiefs of foreign affairs of the Allied nations drew up an agreement at Moscow stating that they would act together in German surrender, disarmament, and control, and that they would support a world organization after the war.

✓   ✓   ✓

The governments of the United States of America, the United Kingdom, the Soviet Union and China:

united in their determination, in accordance with the Declaration by the United Nations of January 1, 1942, and subsequent declarations, to continue hostilities against those Axis powers with which they respectively are at war until such powers have laid down their arms on the basis of unconditional surrender;

conscious of their responsibility to secure the liberation of themselves and the peoples allied with them from the menace of aggression;

[38] *United States Department of State Bulletin, IX, pp. 309-10.*

recognizing the necessity of insuring a rapid and orderly transition from war to peace and of establishing and maintaining international peace and security with the least diversion of the world's human and economic resources for armaments;

jointly declare:

1. That their united action, pledged for the prosecution of the war against their respective enemies, will be continued for the organization and maintenance of peace and security.

2. That those of them at war with a common enemy will act together in all matters relating to the surrender and disarmament of that enemy.

3. That they will take all measures deemed by them to be necessary to provide against any violation of the terms imposed upon the enemy.

4. That they recognise the necessity of establishing at the earliest practicable date a general international organization, based on the principle of the sovereign equality of all peace-loving states, and open to membership by all such states, large and small, for the maintenance of international peace and security.

5. That for the purpose of maintaining international peace and security pending the re-establishment of law and order and the inauguration of a system of general security, they will consult with one another and as occasion requires with other members of the United Nations with a view to joint action on behalf of the community of nations.

6. That after the termination of hostilities they will not employ their military forces within the territories of other states except for the purpose envisaged in this declaration and after joint consultation.

7. That they will confer and cooperate with one another and with other members of the United Nations to bring about a practicable general agreement with respect to the regulation of armaments in the post-war period.

V. Molotov   Cordell Hull
Anthony Eden   Foo Ping-sheung
Moscow,
    30th October, 1943

THE CAIRO CONFERENCE, NOVEMBER 22-26, 1943 [39]

The Cairo Conference, held November 22-26, 1943, brought Generalissimo Chiang Kai-shek into the planning of the big powers, and repeated the major principle of "unconditional surrender" for Japan and Germany.

✓   ✓   ✓

The several military missions have agreed upon future military operations against Japan. The Three Great Allies expressed their resolve to bring unrelenting pressure against their brutal enemies by sea, land, and air. This pressure is already rising.

The Three Great Allies are fighting this war to restrain and punish the aggression of Japan. They covet no gain for themselves and have no thought of territorial expansion. It is their purpose that Japan shall be stripped of all the islands in the Pacific which she has seized or occupied since the beginning of the first World War in 1914, and that all the territories Japan has stolen from the Chinese, such as Manchuria, Formosa, and the Pescadores, shall be restored to the Republic of China. Japan will also be expelled from all other territories which she has taken by violence and greed. The aforesaid three great powers, mindful of the enslavement of the people of Korea, are determined that in due course Korea shall become free and independent.

With these objects in view, the three Allies, in harmony with those of the United Nations at war with Japan, will continue to persevere in the serious and prolonged operations necessary to procure the unconditional surrender of Japan.

[39] *United States Department of State Bulletin,* IX, p. 393.

— 36 —

THE TEHRAN CONFERENCE, DECEMBER 1, 1943 [40]

At the Tehran meeting of Roosevelt, Stalin, and Churchill in November, 1943, the Russians were fully informed of Allied plans for the second-front cross-channel invasion schedule for mid-1944.

✔   ✔   ✔

We—The President of the United States, the Prime Minister of Great Britain, and the Premier of the Soviet Union, have met these four days past, in this, the Capital of our Ally, Iran, and have shaped and confirmed our common policy.

We express our determination that our nations shall work together in war and in the peace that will follow.

As to war—our military staffs have joined in our round table discussions, and we have concerted our plans for the destruction of the German forces. We have reached complete agreement as to the scope and timing of the operations to be undertaken from the east, west and south.

The common understanding which we have here reached guarantees that victory will be ours.

And as to peace—we are sure that our concord will win an enduring Peace. We recognize fully the supreme responsibility resting upon us and all the United Nations to make a peace which will command the goodwill of the overwhelming mass of the peoples of the world and banish the scourge and terror of war for many generations.

With our Diplomatic advisors we have surveyed the problems of the future. We shall seek the cooperation and active participation of all nations, large and small, whose peoples in heart and mind are dedicated, as are our own peoples, to the elimination of tyranny and slavery,

[40] *United States Department of State Bulletin*, IX, pp. 409 ff

oppression and intolerance. We will welcome them, as they may choose to come, into a world family of Democratic Nations.

No power on earth can prevent our destroying the German armies by land, their U Boats by sea, and their war plants from the air.

Our attack will be relentless and increasing.

Emerging from these cordial conferences we look with confidence to the day when all peoples of the world may live free lives, untouched by tyranny, and according to their varying desires and their own consciences.

We came here with hope and determination. We leave here, friends in fact, in spirit and in purpose.

ROOSEVELT, CHURCHILL AND STALIN

Signed at Tehran, *December 1, 1943*

— 37 —

THE SECRET TREATY OF YALTA, FEBRUARY 4-11, 1945 [41]

At Tehran, Stalin assured both Roosevelt and Churchill of his support in the Pacific war. At the Yalta Conference of the Big Three, Stalin demanded territorial concessions in violation of the Atlantic Charter. Roosevelt and Churchill were forced to accept Stalin's terms on the ground of military expediency. The Report of the Yalta Conference was couched in generalities, but a secret treaty was signed by the Big Three without participation of the

[41] *Department of State Press Release*, No. 239, March 24, 1947.

United States State Department and the British Foreign Office. The full text was released by the State Department on March 24, 1947. The agreement was strongly denounced as an unwarranted concession to Stalin enabling him to expand Soviet influence into the heart of Europe and throughout much of North China.

✓ ✓ ✓

Agreement Regarding Japan

The leaders of the three great powers—the Soviet Union, the United States of America, and Great Britain —have agreed that in two or three months after Germany has surrendered and the war in Europe has terminated, the Soviet Union shall enter into the war against Japan on the side of the Allies on condition that:

1. The *status quo* in Outer Mongolia (the Mongolian People's Republic) shall be preserved;

2. The former rights of Russia violated by the treacherous attack of Japan in 1904 shall be restored, viz.:

a. The southern part of Sakhalin as well as the islands adjacent to it shall be returned to the Soviet Union;

b. The commercial port of Dairen shall be internationalized, the preeminent interests of the Soviet Union in this port being safeguarded, and the lease of Port Arthur as a naval base of U.S.S.R. restored;

c. The Chinese Eastern Railroad and the South Manchurian Railroad, which provides an outlet to Dairen, shall be jointly operated by the establishment of a joint Soviet-Chinese company, it being understood that the preeminent interests of the Soviet Union shall be safeguarded and that China shall retain full sovereignty in Manchuria;

3. The Kurile Islands shall be handed over to the Soviet Union. It is understood that the agreement concerning Outer Mongolia and the ports and railroads referred to above will require concurrence of Generalissimo Chiang Kai-shek. The President [*Roosevelt*] will take measures in order to obtain this concurrence on advice from Marshal Stalin.

The heads of the three great powers have agreed that these claims of the Soviet Union shall be unquestionably fulfilled after Japan has been defeated.

For its part, the Soviet Union expresses its readiness to conclude with the National Government of China a pact of friendship and alliance between the U.S.S.R. and China in order to render assistance to China with its armed forces for the purpose of liberating China from the Japanese yoke.

Joseph V. Stalin
Franklin D. Roosevelt
Winston S. Churchill

— 38 —

HITLER'S POLITICAL TESTAMENT, APRIL 29, 1945 [42]

Although he denounced the German people as not worthy of his leadership, Hitler left a political testament, urging them to carry on his ideals.

✔   ✔   ✔

More than thirty years have passed since I made my modest contribution as a volunteer in the First World War, which was forced upon the Reich.

In these three decades, love and loyalty to my people alone have guided me in all my thoughts, actions, and life. They gave me power to make the most difficult decisions which have ever confronted mortal man. I have spent all my time, my powers, and my health in these three decades.

It is untrue that I or anybody else in Germany wanted

[42] *The New York Times,* December 31, 1945.

war in 1939. It was wanted and provoked exclusively by those international statesmen who either were of Jewish origin or worked for Jewish interests. . . .

After six years of war, which, in spite of all setbacks, will one day go down in history as the most glorious and heroic manifestation of the struggle for existence of a nation, I cannot forsake the city that is the capital of this state. As our forces are too small to withstand an enemy attack on this place any longer, and our own resistance will gradually be worn down by men who are merely blind automata, I wish to share my fate with that which millions of others have also taken upon themselves by staying in this town. Further, I shall not fall into the hands of the enemy, who requires a new spectacle, presented by the Jews, to divert their hysterical masses.

I have therefore decided to remain in Berlin and there to choose death voluntarily at that moment when I believe that the position of the Fuehrer and the Chancellery itself can no longer be maintained. I die with a joyful heart in my knowledge of the immeasurable deeds and achievements of our soldiers at the front, of our women at home, the achievements of our peasants and workers and of a contribution unique in history, of our youth that bears my name.

That I express to them all the thanks that come from the bottom of my heart is as clear as my wish that they should therefore not give up the struggle under any circumstances but carry it on wherever they may be against the enemies of the Fatherland, true to the principles of the great Clausewitz.

From the sacrifice of our soldiers and from my own comradeship with them to death itself, the seed has been sown that will grow one day in the history of Germany to the glorious rebirth of the National Socialist movement and thereby to the establishment of a truly united nation. . . .

Before my death, I expel the former Reich Marshal Hermann Goering from the party and withdraw from him all the rights that were conferred on him by the decree of 29 June, 1941, and by my Reichstag speech of the first of September, 1939. . . .

Apart altogether from their disloyalty to me, Goering

and Himmler have brought irreparable shame on the country and the whole nation by secretly negotiating with the enemy without my knowledge and against my will, and also by illegally attempting to seize control of the state.

In order to give the German people a government composed of honorable men who will fulfill the task of continuing the war with all means, as the leader of the nation I appoint the following members of the new Cabinet:

President, Doenitz; Chancellor, Dr. Goebbels; Party Minister, Bormann; Foreign Minister, Seyss-Inquart (*et al.*) . . .

May they finally be conscious that our task, the establishment of a National Socialist State, represents the work of centuries to come and obliges each individual person always to serve the common interest before his own advantage. I ask all Germans, all National Socialists, men, women and all soldiers of the army, to be loyal and obedient to the new Government and its President until death.

Above all, I enjoin the Government of the nation and the people to uphold the racial laws to the limit. . . .

ADMIRAL DOENITZ'S ASSUMPTION OF LEADERSHIP IN THE THIRD REICH, MAY 1, 1945 [43]

Following the suicide of Hitler, leadership of the Third Reich was assumed by Admiral Doenitz with these proclamations.

✓   ✓   ✓

Hamburg Radio Broadcast, May 1, 1945

It is reported from the *Fuehrer's* headquarters that our *Fuehrer*, Adolf Hitler, fighting to the last breath against Bolshevism, fell for Germany this afternoon in his operational headquarters in the Reich Chancellery.

On April 30th the *Fuehrer* appointed Grand Admiral Doenitz his successor. The Grand Admiral and successor of the *Fuehrer* now speaks to the German people.

Doenitz: German men and women, soldiers of the armed forces:

Our *Fuehrer*, Adolf Hitler, has fallen. In the deepest sorrow and respect the German people now . . . The *Fuehrer* has appointed me to be his successor. Fully conscious of the responsibility, I take over the leadership of the German people at this fateful hour. . . .

Admiral Doenitz's "Order of the Day," May 1, 1945

German armed forces, my comrades: The *Fuehrer* has fallen. Faithful to his great ideal to save the nations of Europe from Bolshevism, he has given his life and has met a hero's death. In him one of the greatest heroes of German history has departed. With proud respect and grief we lower our standards.

[43] *The New York Times,* May 2, 1945.

The *Fuehrer* has designated me to be the head of the State and Supreme Commander. . . . I am resolved to continue the struggle against the Bolsheviks. . . . Against the British and Americans I am bound to continue to fight as far and as long as they impede me in the struggle against Bolshevism. . . . For every single one of you the oath of loyalty to the *Fuehrer* is transferred straight to my person as the *Fuehrer's* appointed successor.

German soldiers! Do your duty! The existence of our people is at stake.

— 40 —

THE POTSDAM DECLARATION, AUGUST 2, 1945[44]

At the last wartime conference, held at Potsdam from July 17 to August 2, 1945, the new Big Three (Stalin, Attlee, and Truman) set down the terms for a defeated Germany, decided the question of reparations, and handed over Koenigsberg and the eastern part of East Prussia to the Soviet Union. Since it was not known how much time and blood would be required to defeat Japan, the United States and Great Britain continued the policy of capitulating to Stalin's wishes.

✓   ✓   ✓

I. Report on the Tripartite Conference of Berlin

On July 17, 1945, the President of the United States of America, Harry S. Truman; the Chairman of the Council of People's Commissars of the Union of Soviet Socialist Republics, Generalissimo J. V. Stalin, and the Prime Minister of Great Britain, Winston S. Churchill, together with Mr. Clement R. Attlee, met in the Tripartite Conference of Berlin. They were accompanied by the Foreign Secretaries of the three Governments, Mr. James F. Byrnes, Mr. V. M. Molotoff, and Mr. Anthony Eden, the Chief of Staff, and other advisers.

There were nine meetings between July 17 and July 25. The Conference was then interrupted for two days

[44] *The New York Times,* August 3, 1945.

while the results of the British general election were being declared.

On July 28 Mr. Attlee returned to the Conference as Prime Minister, accompanied by the new Secretary of State for Foreign Affairs, Mr. Ernest Bevin. . . .

The meetings of the Conference were held at the Cecilienhof, near Potsdam. The Conference ended on Aug. 2, 1945. . . .

President Truman, Generalissimo Stalin and Prime Minister Attlee leave this Conference, which has strengthened the ties between the three Governments and extended the scope of their collaboration and understanding, with renewed confidence that their Governments and peoples, together with the other United Nations, will insure the creation of a just and enduring peace.

II. Establishment of a Council of Foreign Ministers

The Conference reached an agreement for the establishment of a Council of Foreign Ministers representing the five principal powers to continue the necessary preparatory work for the peace settlements and to take up other matters which from time to time may be referred to the Council by agreement of the Governments participating in the Conference. . . .

III. Germany

The Allied armies are in occupation of the whole of Germany and the German people have begun to atone for the terrible crimes committed under the leadership of those whom in the hour of their success, they openly approved and blindly obeyed.

Agreement has been reached at this conference on the political and economic principles of a coordinated Allied policy toward defeated Germany during the period of Allied control.

The purpose of this agreement is to carry out the Crimea Declaration on Germany. German militarism and nazism will be extirpated and the Allies will take in agreement together, now and in the future, the other measures necessary to assure that Germany never again will threaten her neighbors or the peace of the world.

It is not the intention of the Allies to destroy or enslave the German people. It is the intention of the Allies that the German people be given the opportunity to prepare for the eventual reconstruction of their life on a democratic and peaceful basis. If their own efforts are steadily directed to this end, it will be possible for them in due course to take their place among the free and peaceful peoples of the world.

The text of the agreement is as follows:

The political and economic principles to govern the treatment of Germany in the initial control period.

A. POLITICAL PRINCIPLES

1. In accordance with the agreement on control machinery in Germany, supreme authority in Germany is exercised on instructions from their respective Governments, by the Commanders in Chief of the Armed Forces of the United States of America, the United Kingdom, the Union of Soviet Socialist Republics, and the French Republic, each in his own zone of occupation, and also jointly, in matters affecting Germany as a whole, in their capacity as members of the Control Council.

2. So far as is practicable, there shall be uniformity of treatment of the German population throughout Germany.

3. The purposes of the occupation of Germany by which the Control Council shall be guided are:

(I) The complete disarmament and demilitarization of Germany and the elimination or control of all German industry that could be used for military production. To these ends:

(A) All German land, naval and air forces, the S.S., S.A., S.D., and Gestapo, with all their organizations, staffs and institutions, including the general staff, the officers' corps, reserve corps, military schools, war veterans' organizations and all other military and quasi-military organizations, together with all clubs and associations which serve to keep alive the military tradition in Germany, shall be completely and finally abolished in such manner as permanently to prevent the revival or reorganization of German militarism and nazism.

(B) All arms, ammunition and implements of war and all specialized facilities for their production shall be held at the disposal of the Allies or destroyed. The maintenance and production of all aircraft and all arms, ammunition and implements of war shall be prevented.

(II) To convince the German people that they have suffered a total military defeat and that they cannot escape responsibility for what they have brought upon themselves, since their own ruthless warfare and the fanatical Nazi resistance have destroyed German economy and made chaos and suffering inevitable.

(III) To destroy the National Socialist Party and its affiliated and supervised organizations, to dissolve all Nazi institutions, to insure that they are not revived in any form, and to prevent all Nazi and militarist activity or propaganda.

(IV) To prepare for the eventual reconstruction of German political life on a democratic basis and for eventual peaceful cooperation in international life by Germany.

4. All Nazi laws which provided the basis of the Hitler regime or established discrimination on grounds of race, creed, or political opinion shall be abolished. No such discriminations, whether legal, administrative or otherwise, shall be tolerated.

5. War criminals and those who have participated in planning or carrying out Nazi enterprises involving or resulting in atrocities or war crimes shall be arrested and brought to judgment. Nazi leaders, influential Nazi supporters and high officials of Nazi organizations and institutions and any other persons dangerous to the occupation or its objectives shall be arrested and interned.

6. All members of the Nazi party who have been more than nominal participants in its activities and all other persons hostile to Allied purposes shall be removed from public and semi-public office and from positions of responsibility in important private undertakings. Such persons shall be replaced by persons who, by their political and moral qualities, are deemed capable of assisting in developing genuine democratic institutions in Germany.

7. German education shall be so controlled as completely to eliminate Nazi and militarist doctrines and to make possible the successful development of democratic ideas.

8. The judicial system will be reorganized in accordance with the principles of democracy, of justice under law, and of equal rights for all citizens without distinction of race, nationality or religion.

9. The administration of affairs in Germany should be directed toward the decentralization of the political structure and the development of local responsibility. . . .

B. ECONOMIC PRINCIPLES

11. In order to eliminate Germany's war potential, the production of arms, ammunition and implements of war as well as all types of aircraft and sea-going ships shall be prohibited and prevented. Production of metals, chemicals, machinery and other items that are directly necessary to a war economy shall be rigidly controlled and restricted to Germany's approved post-war peacetime needs to meet the objectives stated in Paragraph 15. Productive capacity not needed for permitted production shall be removed in accordance with the reparations plan recommended by the Allied Commission on reparations and approved by the Governments concerned, or if not removed shall be destroyed.

12. At the earliest practicable date the German economy shall be decentralized for the purpose of eliminating the present excessive concentration of economic power as exemplified in particular by cartels, syndicates, trusts and other monopolistic arrangements.

13. In organizing the German economy, primary emphasis shall be given to the development of agriculture and peaceful domestic industries.

14. During the period of occupation Germany shall be treated as a single economic unit. To this end common policies shall be established in regard to:

    (A) Mining and industrial production and allocations;

    (B) Agriculture, forestry and fishing;

    (C) Wages, prices and rationing;

    (D) Import and export program for Germany as a whole;

    (E) Currency and banking, central taxation and customs;

(F) Reparation and removal of industrial war potential;

(G) Transportation and communications.

In applying these policies account shall be taken, where appropriate, of varying local conditions.

15. Allied controls shall be imposed upon the German economy, but only to the extent necessary;

(A) To carry out programs of industrial disarmament and demilitarization, of reparations, and of approved exports and imports. . . .

IV. Reparations from Germany

In accordance with the Crimea decision that Germany be compelled to compensate to the greatest possible extent for the loss and suffering that she has caused to the United Nations and for which the German people cannot escape responsibility, the following agreement on reparations was reached:

1. Reparation claims of the U.S.S.R. shall be met by removals from the zone of Germany occupied by the U.S.S.R. and from appropriate German external assets.

2. The U.S.S.R. undertakes to settle the reparation claims of Poland from its own share of reparations.

3. The reparation claims of the United States, the United Kingdom and other countries entitled to reparations shall be met from the western zones and from appropriate German external assets. . . .

VII. War Criminals

The three Governments have taken note of the discussions which have been proceeding in recent weeks in London between British, United States, Soviet and French representatives with a view to reaching agreement on the methods of trial of those major war criminals whose crimes under the Moscow Declaration of October, 1943, have no particular geographical localization. . . .

X. Conclusion of Peace Treaties and Admission to the United Nations Organization

The Conference agreed upon the following statement of common policy for establishing, as soon as possible, the conditions of lasting peace after victory in Europe:

The three Governments consider it desirable that the present anomalous position of Italy, Bulgaria, Finland, Hungary and Rumania should be terminated by the conclusion of peace treaties. They trust that the other interested Allied Governments will share these views.

For their part, the three Governments have included the preparation of a peace treaty for Italy as the first among the immediate important tasks to be undertaken by the new Council of Foreign Ministers. Italy was the first of the Axis powers to break with Germany, to whose defeat she has made a material contribution, and has now joined with the Allies in the struggle against Japan. . . .

XI. TERRITORIAL TRUSTEESHIPS

The Conference examined a proposal by the Soviet Government concerning trusteeship territories as defined in the decision of the Crimea Conference and in the Charter of the United Nations Organization.

After an exchange of views on this question it was decided that the disposition of any former Italian territories was one to be decided in connection with the preparation of a peace treaty for Italy and that the question of Italian territory would be considered by the September council of Ministers of Foreign Affairs.

XII. REVISED ALLIED CONTROL COMMISSION PROCEDURE IN RUMANIA, BULGARIA, AND HUNGARY

The three Governments took note that the Soviet representatives on the Allied Control Commissions in Rumania, Bulgaria and Hungary have communicated to their United Kingdom and United States colleagues proposals for improving the work of the control commission, now that hostilities in Europe have ceased. . . .

XIII. ORDERLY TRANSFERS OF GERMAN POPULATIONS

The Conference reached the following agreement on the removal of Germans from Poland, Czechoslovakia and Hungary:

The three Governments, having considered the question in all its aspects, recognize that the transfer to Germany of German populations, or elements thereof, remaining in Poland, Czechoslovakia and Hungary, will have to be undertaken. They agree that any transfers that take place should be effected in an orderly and humane manner. . . .

XIV. MILITARY TALKS

During the conference there were meetings between the Chiefs of Staff of the three Governments on military matters of common interest.

Approved:

> J. V. STALIN
> HARRY S. TRUMAN
> C. R. ATTLEE

— 41 —

THE JAPANESE INSTRUMENT OF SURRENDER, SEPTEMBER 2, 1945 [45]

The Japanese Instrument of Surrender was formally signed in Tokyo Bay aboard the U.S.S. *Missouri* on September 2, 1945, in the presence of Allied representatives led by General MacArthur.

✓   ✓   ✓

We, acting by command of and in behalf of the Emperor of Japan, the Japanese Government and the Japanese Imperial General Headquarters, hereby accept the provisions set forth in the declaration issued by the heads of the Governments of the United States, China and Great Britain on 26 July, 1945, at Potsdam, and subsequently adhered to by the Union of Soviet Socialist Republics, which four powers are hereafter referred to as the Allied Powers.

We hereby proclaim the unconditional surrender to the Allied Powers of the Japanese Imperial General Headquarters and of all Japanese armed forces and all armed forces under Japanese control wherever situated.

We hereby command all Japanese forces wherever situated and the Japanese people to cease hostilities forthwith, to preserve and save from damage all ships, aircraft, and military and civil property and to comply with all requirements which may be imposed by the Supreme

[45] *United States Department of State Bulletin,* XIII (September 9, 1945), pp. 364-65.

Commander for the Allied Powers or by agencies of the Japanese Government at his direction. . . .

We hereby command all civil, military and naval officials to obey and enforce all proclamations, orders and directives deemed by the Supreme Commander for the Allied Powers to be proper to effectuate this surrender and issued by him or under his authority. . . .

We hereby undertake for the Emperor, the Japanese Government and their successors to carry out the provisions of the Potsdam Declaration in good faith. . . .

We hereby command the Japanese Imperial Government and the Japanese Imperial General Headquarters at once to liberate all allied prisoners of war and civilian internees now under Japanese control and to provide for their protection, care, maintenance and immediate transportation to places as directed.

The authority of the Emperor and the Japanese Government to rule the state shall be subject to the Supreme Commander for the Allied Powers who will take such steps as he deems proper to effectuate these terms of surrender.

> Signed at Tokyo Bay, Japan at 0904 I on the Second day of September, 1945
>
> (Signed) Mamoru Shigemitsu, By Command and in behalf of the Emperor of Japan and the Japanese Government
>
> (Signed) Yoshijiro Umezu, By Command and in behalf of the Japanese Imperial General Headquarters

Accepted at Tokyo Bay, Japan at 0908 I on the Second day of September, 1945, for the United States, Republic of China, United Kingdom and the Union of Soviet Socialist Republics, and in the interests of other United Nations at war with Japan.

> Douglas MacArthur, Supreme Commander
> for the Allied Powers

[*The signatures of representatives of the United States, China, Great Britain, Russia, Australia, Canada, France, the Netherlands, and New Zealand follow.*]

— 42 —

THE BARUCH PROPOSALS FOR THE CONTROL OF ATOMIC ENERGY, JUNE, 1946 [46]

The Atomic Energy Commission of the United Nations held its first meeting in New York in June, 1946. The American representative on the commission, Bernard M. Baruch (1870-   ), presented the official American policy for the control of atomic energy. The following excerpts give the fundamental features of the Baruch Plan. The Soviet representative, Gromyko, countered the American proposals by a plan calling for a prior step, the conclusion of a rigid international agreement to prohibit the use of atomic weapons and to destroy all existing weapons within three months. Furthermore, the Soviet Union objected to the Baruch idea of inspection, calling, instead, for an inspectorial apparatus "within the framework of the Security Council," where it would be subject to the Soviet veto. Soviet Russia did not desire to be "invaded" by an army of inspectors with rights of free and unhampered travel within the Soviet Union; her representatives were unimpressed with the arguments that this inspection would be applied to all states alike. An agreement on international control of atomic energy became impossible in the face of Soviet Russia's almost pathological suspicion of the West.

[46] United States Department of State, *The United States and the United Nations*, Report Series No. 7 (Washington, 1947), pp. 169-78.

My Fellow Members of the United Nations Atomic Energy Commission, and My Fellow Citizens of the World:

We are here to make a choice between the quick and the dead.

That is our business.

Behind the black portent of the new atomic age lies a hope which, seized upon with faith, can work our salvation. If we fail, then we have damned every man to be the slave of Fear. Let us not deceive ourselves: We must elect World Peace or World Destruction.

Science has torn from nature a secret so vast in its potentialities that our minds cower in fear from the terror it creates. Yet terror is not enough to inhibit the use of the atomic bomb. The terror created by weapons has never stopped man from employing them. For each new weapon a defense has been produced, in time. But now we face a condition in which adequate defense does not exist.

Science, which gave us this dread power, shows that it can be made a giant help to humanity, but science does *not* show us how to prevent its baleful use. So we have been appointed to obviate that peril by finding a meeting of the minds and hearts of our people. Only in the will of mankind lies the answer.

It is to express this will and make it effective that we have been assembled. We must provide the mechanisms to assure that atomic energy is used for peaceful purposes and preclude its use in war. To that end, we must provide immediate, swift, and sure punishment of those who violate the agreements that are reached by the nations. Penalization is essential if peace is to be more than a feverish interlude between wars. . . .

I now submit the following measures as representing the fundamental features of a plan which could give effect to certain of the conclusions which I have epitomized.

1. *General.* The Authority should set up a thorough plan for control of the field of atomic energy, through various forms of ownership, dominion, licenses, operation, inspection, research, and management by competent personnel. After this is provided for, there should be as little interference as may be with the economic plans and the

present private, corporate, and state relationships in the several countries involved.

2. *Raw Materials.* The Authority should have as one of its earliest purposes to obtain and maintain complete and accurate information on world supplies of uranium and thorium and to bring them under its dominion. The precise pattern of control for various types of deposits of such materials will have to depend upon the geological, mining, refining, and economic facts involved in different situations.

The Authority should conduct continuous surveys so that it will have the most complete knowledge of the world geology of uranium and thorium. Only after all current information on world sources of uranium and thorium is known to us all can equitable plans be made for their production, refining, and distribution.

3. *Primary Production Plants.* The Authority should exercise complete managerial control of the production of fissionable materials. This means that it should control and operate all plants producing fissionable materials in dangerous quantities and must own and control the product of these plants.

4. *Atomic Explosives.* The Authority should be given sole and exclusive right to conduct research in the field of atomic explosives. Research activities in the field of atomic explosives are essential in order that the Authority may keep in the forefront of knowledge in the field of atomic energy and fulfil the objective of preventing illicit manufacture of bombs. Only by maintaining its position as the best-informed agency will the Authority be able to determine the line between intrinsically dangerous and non-dangerous activities.

5. *Strategic Distribution of Activities and Materials.* The activities entrusted to the Authority because they are intrinsically dangerous to security should be distributed throughout the world. Similarly, stockpiles of raw materials and fissionable materials should not be centralized.

6. *Non-dangerous Activities.* A function of the Authority should be promotion of the peacetime benefits of atomic energy.

Atomic research (except in explosives), the use of research reactors, the production of radioactive tracers by means of non-dangerous reactors, the use of such tracers, and to some extent the production of power should be open to nations and their citizens under reasonable licensing arrangements from the Authority. Denatured materials, whose use we know also requires suitable safeguards, should be furnished for such purposes by the Authority under lease or other arrangement. Denaturing seems to have been overestimated by the public as a safety measure.

7. *Definition of Dangerous and Non-dangerous Activities.* Although a reasonable dividing line can be drawn between dangerous and non-dangerous activities, it is not hard and fast. Provision should, therefore, be made to assure constant reexamination of the questions and to permit revision of the dividing line as changing conditions and new discoveries may require.

8. *Operations of Dangerous Activities.* Any plant dealing with uranium and thorium after it once reaches the potential of dangerous use must be not only subject to the most rigorous and competent inspection by the Authority, but its actual operation shall be under the management, supervision, and control of that authority.

9. *Inspection.* By assigning intrinsically dangerous activities exclusively to the Authority, the difficulties of inspection are reduced. If the Authority is the only agency which may lawfully conduct dangerous activities, then visible operation by others than the Authority will constitute an unambiguous danger signal. Inspection will also occur in connection with the licensing function of the Authority.

10. *Freedom of Access.* Adequate ingress and egress for all qualified representatives of the Authority must be assured. Many of the inspection activities of the Authority should grow out of, and be incidental to, its other functions. Important measures of inspection will be associated with the tight control of raw materials, for this is a keynote of the plan. The continuing activities of prospecting, survey, and research in relation to raw materials will be designed not only to serve the affirmative development functions of the authority but also to assure that no surreptitious operations are conducted in the raw-material field by nation or their citizens.

11. *Personnel.* The personnel of the Authority should be recruited on a basis of proven competence but also as far as possible on an international basis.

12. *Progress by Stages.* A primary step in the creation of the system of control is the setting forth, in comprehensive terms, of the functions, responsibilities, powers, and limitations of the Authority. Once a charter for the Authority has been adopted, the Authority and the system of control for which it will be responsible will require time to become fully organized and effective. The plan of control will, therefore, have to come into effect in successive stages. These should be specifically fixed in the charter or means should otherwise be set forth in the charter for transitions from one stage to another, as contemplated in the resolution of the United Nations Assembly which created this Commission.

13. *Disclosures.* In the deliberations of the United Nations Commission on Atomic Energy, the United States is prepared to make available the information essential to a reasonable understanding of the proposals which it advocates. Further disclosures must be dependent, in the interests of all, upon the effective ratification of the treaty. When the Authority is actually created, the United States will join the other nations in making available the further information essential to that organization for the performance of its functions. As the successive stages of international control are reached, the United States will be prepared to yield, to the extent required by each stage, national control of the activities in this field to the Authority.

14. *International Control.* There will be questions about the extent of control to be allowed to national bodies, when the Authority is established. Purely national authorities for control and development of atomic energy should to the extent necessary for the effective operation of the Authority be subordinate to it. This is neither an endorsement nor a disapproval of the creation of national authorities. The Commission should evolve a clear demarcation of the scope of duties and responsibilities of such national authorities. . . .

— 43 —

EXTRACTS FROM THE NUREMBERG TRIAL JUDGMENTS, OCTOBER 1, 1946 [47]

The public trial of twenty-two Nazi leaders began at Nuremberg in November, 1945. Although special courts had been set up in the past to judge political crimes by extraordinary authority, no such court had ever obtained such universal recognition. Here was in effect the first step in the creation of an international court to judge crimes against peace, against humanity, and against defenseless minorities. The legality of the proceedings troubled many jurists, who were disturbed by the *ex post facto* implications of the trials. But when it became clear from the carefully compiled testimony of the court how mercilessly the Nazi leaders had treated their victims, fewer and fewer voices were raised against the proceedings. The evidence showed that between five and ten million people had been starved, beaten, and tortured to death in concentration camps, a crime without parallel in history.

"Tod durch den Strang!"—"Death by the rope!" This was the verdict for eleven of the defendants: Goering (age 52), Ribbentrop (53), Keitel (63), Kaltenbrunner (43), Rosenberg (53), Frank (46), Frick (69), Streicher (61), Sauckel (48), Jodl (56), and Seyss-Inquart

[47] Condensed from the official text in *Trial of the Major War Criminals before The International Military Tribunal* (Nuremberg, 1948), XXII, pp. 524-33, 539-41, 552-56, 556-71.

(54). Bormann (45), *in absentia,* was also sentenced to death. Three others were sent to prison for life—Hess (52), Funk (56), and Raeder (70). Four were condemned to terms of imprisonment—Doenitz (55) to 10 years, Shirach (39) to 20 years, Neurath (72) to 15 years, and Speer (40) to 20 years. Three were acquitted —Schacht (69), von Papen (66) and Fritsche (46). Extracts from the verdicts follow.

The four counts of the indictment:

1. Conspiracy to commit crimes alleged in other counts;
2. Crimes against peace;
3. War crimes;
4. Crimes against humanity.

GOERING: From the moment he joined the party in 1922 and took command of the street fighting organization, the SA, Goering was the adviser, the active agent of Hitler and one of the prime leaders of the Nazi movement. As Hitler's political deputy he was largely instrumental in bringing the National Socialists to power in 1933, and was charged with consolidating this power and expanding the German armed might. He developed the Gestapo and created the first concentration camps, relinquishing them to Himmler in 1934; conducted the Roehm purge in that year and engineered the sordid proceedings which resulted in the removal of von Blomberg and von Fritsch from the army. . . .

Goering commanded the Luftwaffe in the attack on Poland and throughout the aggressive wars which followed. . . . The record is filled with Goering's admissions of his complicity in the use of slave labor. . . .

Goering persecuted the Jews, particularly after the November, 1938 riots, and not only in Germany, where he raised the billion mark fine as stated elsewhere, but in the conquered territories as well. His own utterances, then and in his testimony, show his interest was primarily economic—how to get their property and how to force them out of the economic life of Europe. . . .

There is nothing to be said in mitigation. . . . His guilt is unique in its enormity. The record discloses no excuse for this man.

VERDICT: GUILTY on all 4 counts.

SENTENCE: Death by hanging.

HESS: . . . As deputy to the *Fuehrer*, Hess was the top man in the Nazi party with responsibility for handling all Party matters and authority to make decisions in Hitler's name on all questions of Party leadership. . . . Hess was an informed and willing participant in German aggression against Austria, Czechoslovakia, and Poland. . . . With him on his flight to England, Hess carried certain peace proposals which he alleged Hitler was prepared to accept. It is significant to note that this flight took place only ten days after the date on which Hitler fixed the time for attacking the Soviet Union. . . .

That Hess acts in an abnormal manner, suffers from loss of memory, and has mentally deteriorated during this trial, may be true. But there is nothing to show that he does not realize the nature of the charges against him, or is incapable of defending himself. He was ably represented at the trial by counsel, appointed for that purpose by the Tribunal. There is no suggestion that Hess was not completely sane when the acts charged against him were committed.

VERDICT: GUILTY on counts 1 and 2.

SENTENCE: Life imprisonment.

ROSENBERG: Recognized as the Party's ideologist, he developed and spread Nazi doctrines in the newspapers *Völkischer Beobachter* and *NS Monatshefte*, which he edited, and in the numerous books he wrote. . . .

Rosenberg bears a major responsibility for the formulation and execution of occupation policies in the Occupied Eastern territories. . . . On July 17, 1941, Hitler appointed Rosenberg Reich Minister of the Eastern Occupied Territories, and publicly charged him with responsibility for civil administration. . . . He helped to formulate the policies of Germanization, exploitation, forced labor, extermination of Jews and opponents of Nazi rule, and he set up an administration which carried them out. . . . His subordinates engaged in mass killings of Jews, and his civil administrators considered that cleansing the Eastern Occupied Territories of Jews was necessary. . . . His signature of approval appears on the order of June 14, 1941, for the *Heu Aktion*, the apprehension of 40,000 to 50,000 youths, aged 10-14, for shipment to the Reich. . . .

VERDICT: GUILTY on all 4 counts.

SENTENCE: Death by hanging.

RIBBENTROP: Ribbentrop was not present at the Hossbach Conference held on November 5, 1937, but on January 2, 1938, while Ambassador to England, he sent a memorandum to Hitler indicating his opinion that a change in the status quo in the East in the German sense could only be carried out by force and suggesting methods to prevent England and France from intervening in a European war fought to bring about such a change. . . . Ribbentrop participated in the aggressive plans against Czechoslovakia. Beginning in March, 1938, he was in close touch with the Sudeten German Party and gave them instructions which had the effect of keeping the Sudeten German question a live issue which might serve as an excuse for the attack which Germany was planning against Czechoslovakia. . . .

Ribbentrop played a particularly significant rôle in the diplomatic activity which led up to the attack on Poland. He participated in a conference held on August 12, 1939, for the purpose of obtaining Italian support if the attack should lead to a general European war. . . .

He played an important part in Hitler's "final solution" of the Jewish question. In September, 1942, he ordered the German diplomatic representatives accredited to various satellites to hasten deportation of the Jews to the East. . . . It was because Hitler's policy and plans coincided with his own ideas that Ribbentrop served him so willingly to the end.

VERDICT: GUILTY on all 4 counts.

SENTENCE: Death by hanging.

JODL: . . . Jodl discussed the Norway invasion with Hitler, Keitel, and Raeder on December 12, 1939; his diary is replete with late entries on his activities in preparing this attack. . . . He was active in the planning against Greece and Yugoslavia. . . . His defense, in brief, is the doctrine of "superior orders," prohibited by Article VIII of the Charter as a defense. There is nothing in mitigation. Participation in such crimes as these has never been required of any soldier and he cannot now shield himself behind a mythical requirement of soldierly obedience at all costs as his excuse for commission of these crimes.

VERDICT: GUILTY on all 4 counts.

SENTENCE: Death by hanging.

SCHACHT: Schacht was an active supporter of the Nazi Party before its accession to power on January 30, 1933, and supported the appointment of Hitler to the post of Chancellor. After that he played an important rôle in the vigorous rearmament program which was adopted, using the facilities of the Reichsbank to the fullest extent in the German rearmament effort. . . . As Minister of Economics and as Plenipotentiary General for War Economy he was active in organizing the German economy for war. . . . But rearmament of itself is not criminal under the Charter. . . . The Tribunal has considered the whole of this evidence with great care, and comes to the conclusion that this necessary inference has not been established beyond a reasonable doubt.

VERDICT: NOT GUILTY.

— 44 —

THE TRUMAN DOCTRINE, MARCH 12, 1947 [48]

The end of World War II found Soviet Russia gradually extending its power into the Balkans and the Near and Middle East. Russian pressure on Greece, Turkey, and Iran aroused alarm in the West. Great Britain had been the traditional strong power in this area, but the decline of British power, resulting from the war, obliged the United States to define its position. In March, 1947, in Washington, President Truman enunciated the policy called after him the Truman Doctrine. In May Congress passed the Greek-Turkish Act. The Truman Doctrine put a stop to further Russian expansion in the area. President Truman's address to Congress is reprinted here.

✓   ✓   ✓

The gravity of the situation which confronts the world today necessitates my appearance before a joint session of the Congress.

The foreign policy and the national security of this country are involved.

One aspect of the present situation, which I wish to present to you at this time for your consideration and decision, concerns Greece and Turkey.

The United States has received from the Greek government an urgent appeal for financial and economic assistance. Preliminary reports from the American economic

[48] *Congressional Record,* XCIII (March 12, 1947), pp. 1999-2000.

mission now in Greece and reports from the American Ambassador in Greece corroborate the statement of the Greek government that assistance is imperative if Greece is to survive as a free nation.

I do not believe that the American people and the Congress wish to turn a deaf ear to the appeal of the Greek government.

Greece is not a rich country. Lack of sufficient resources has always forced the Greek people to work hard to make both ends meet. Since 1940 this industrious and peace-loving country has suffered invasion, four years of cruel enemy occupation and bitter internal strife.

When forces of liberation entered Greece they found that the retreating Germans had destroyed virtually all the railways, roads, port facilities, communications and merchant marine. More than a thousand villages had been burned. Eighty-five per cent of the children were tubercular. Livestock, poultry and draft animals had almost disappeared. Inflation had wiped out practically all savings.

As a result of these tragic conditions, a militant minority, exploiting human want and misery, was able to create political chaos, which, until now, has made economic recovery impossible. Greece is today without funds to finance the importation of those goods which are essential to bare subsistence. Under these circumstances the people of Greece cannot make progress in solving their problems of reconstruction. Greece is in desperate need of financial and economic assistance to enable it to resume purchases of food, clothing, fuel and seeds. These are indispensable for subsistence of its people and are obtainable only from abroad. Greece must have help to import the goods necessary to restore internal order and security so essential for economic and political recovery.

The Greek government has also asked for the assistance of experienced American administrators, economists and technicians to insure that the financial and other aid given Greece shall be used effectively in creating a stable and self-sustaining economy and in improving its public administration.

The very existence of the Greek state is today threatened by the terrorist activities of several thousand armed men, led by Communists, who defy the government's authority at a number of points, particularly along the northern boundaries. A commission appointed by the United Nations Security Council is at present investigating disturbed conditions in northern Greece on the one hand and Albania, Bulgaria and Yugoslavia on the other.

Meanwhile, the Greek government is unable to cope with the situation. The Greek army is small and poorly equipped. It needs supplies and equipment if it is to restore the authority of the government throughout Greek territory.

Greece must have assistance if it is to become a self-supporting and self-respecting democracy.

The United States must supply that assistance. We have already extended to Greece certain types of relief and economic aid but they are inadequate.

There is no other country to which democratic Greece can turn.

No other nation is willing and able to provide the necessary support for a democratic Greek government.

The British government, which has been helping Greece, can give no further financial or economic aid after March 31. Great Britain finds itself under the necessity of reducing or liquidating its commitments in several parts of the world, including Greece.

We have considered how the United Nations might assist in this crisis. But the situation is an urgent one requiring immediate action, and the United Nations and its related organizations are not in a position to extend help of the kind that is required.

It is important to note that the Greek government has asked for our aid in utilizing effectively the financial and other assistance we may give to Greece, and in improving its public administration. It is of the utmost importance that we supervise the use of any funds made available to Greece, in such a manner that each dollar spent will count toward making Greece self-supporting, and will help to build an economy in which a healthy democracy can flourish.

No government is perfect. One of the chief virtues of a democracy, however, is that its defects are always visible and under democratic processes can be pointed out and corrected. The government of Greece is not perfect. Nevertheless it represents 80 per cent of the members of the Greek Parliament who were chosen in an election last year. Foreign observers, including 692 Americans, considered this election to be a fair expression of the views of the Greek people.

The Greek government has been operating in an atmosphere of chaos and extremism. It has made mistakes. The extension of aid by this country does not mean that the United States condones everything that the Greek government has done or will do. We have condemned in the past, and we condemn now, extremist measures of the Right or the Left. We have in the past advised tolerance, and we advise tolerance now.

Greece's neighbor, Turkey, also deserves our attention.

The future of Turkey as an independent and economically sound state is clearly no less important to the freedom-loving people of the world than the future of Greece. The circumstances in which Turkey finds itself today are considerably different from those of Greece. Turkey has been spared the disasters that have beset Greece. And during the war the United States and Great Britain furnished Turkey with material aid. Nevertheless, Turkey now needs our support.

Since the war, Turkey has sought financial assistance from Great Britain and the United States for the purpose of effecting that modernization necessary for the maintenance of its national integrity.

That integrity is essential for the preservation of order in the Middle East.

The British government has informed us that, owing to its own difficulties, it can no longer extend financial or economic aid to Turkey.

As in the case of Greece, if Turkey is to have the assistance it needs, the United States must supply it. We are the only country that can supply that help.

I am fully aware of the broad implications involved if the United States extends assistance to Greece and Turkey, and I shall discuss these implications with you at this time.

One of the primary objectives of the foreign policy of the United States is the creation of conditions in which we and other nations of the world will be able to work out a way of life free from coercion. This was a fundamental issue in the war with Germany and Japan. Our victory was won over countries which sought to impose their will, and their way of life, upon other nations.

To ensure the peaceful development of nations, free from coercion, the United States has taken a leading part in establishing the United Nations. The United Nations is designed to make possible lasting freedom and independence for all its members. We shall not realize our objectives, however, unless we are willing to help free people to maintain their free institutions and their national integrity against aggressive movements that seek to impose upon them totalitarian regimes. This is no more than a frank recognition that totalitarian regimes imposed on free peoples, by direct or indirect aggression, undermine the foundations of international peace and hence the security of the United States.

The peoples of a number of countries of the world have recently had totalitarian regimes forced upon them against their will. The government of the United States has made frequent protests against coercion and intimidation, in violation of the Yalta agreement, in Poland, Rumania and Bulgaria. I must also state that in a number of other countries there have been similar developments.

At the present moment in world history nearly every nation must choose between alternative ways of life. The choice is too often not a free one.

One way of life is based upon the will of the majority, and is distinguished by free institutions, representative government, free elections, guaranties of individual liberty, freedom of speech and religion and freedom from political oppression.

The second way of life is based upon the will of a minority forcibly imposed upon the majority. It relies upon terror and oppression, a controlled press and radio, fixed elections and the suppression of personal freedom.

I believe that it must be the policy of the United States to support peoples who are resisting attempted subjugation by armed minorities or by outside pressures.

I believe that we must assist free peoples to work out their own destinies in their own way.

I believe that our help should be primarily through economic and financial aid which is essential to economic stability and orderly political processes.

The world is not static, and the status quo is not sacred. But we cannot allow change in the status quo in violation of the charter of the United Nations by such methods as coercion, or by such subterfuges as political infiltration. In helping free and independent nations to maintain their freedom, the United States will be giving effect to the principles of the charter of the United Nations.

It is necessary only to glance at a map to realize that the survival and integrity of the Greek nation are of grave importance in a much wider situation. If Greece should fall under the control of an armed minority, the effect upon its neighbor, Turkey, would be immediate and serious. Confusion and disorder might well spread throughout the entire Middle East.

Moreover, the disappearance of Greece as an independent state would have a profound effect upon those countries in Europe whose people are struggling against great difficulties to maintain their freedoms and their independence while they repair the damages of war.

It would be an unspeakable tragedy if these countries, which have struggled so long against overwhelming odds, should lose that victory for which they have sacrificed so much. Collapse of free institutions and loss of independence would be disastrous not only for them but for the world. Discouragement and possibly failure would quickly be the lot of neighboring peoples striving to maintain their freedom and independence.

Should we fail to aid Greece and Turkey in this fateful hour, the effect will be far-reaching to the West as well as to the East.

I therefore ask the Congress to provide authority for assistance to Greece and Turkey in the amount of $400,-000,000 for the period ending June 30, 1948. In requesting these funds, I have taken into consideration the maximum amount of relief assistance which would be furnished to Greece out of the $350,000,000 which I recently requested that the Congress authorize for the prevention of starvation and suffering in countries devastated by the war.

In addition to funds, I ask the Congress to authorize the detail of American civilian and military personnel to Greece and Turkey, at the request of those countries, to assist in the tasks of reconstruction, and for the purpose of supervising the use of such financial and material assistance as may be furnished. I recommend that authority be provided for the instruction and training of selected Greek and Turkish personnel.

Finally, I ask that the Congress provide authority which will permit the speediest and most effective use, in terms of needed commodities, supplies and equipment, of such funds as may be authorized.

If further funds, or further authority, should be needed for purposes indicated in this message, I shall not hesitate to bring the situation before Congress. On this subject the executive and legislative branches of the government must work together.

This is a serious course upon which we embark.

I would not recommend it except that the alternative is much more serious.

The United States contributed $341,000,000,000 toward winning World War II. This is an investment in world freedom and world peace.

The assistance that I am recommending for Greece and Turkey amounts to little more than one-tenth of 1 per cent of this investment. It is only common sense that we should safeguard this investment and make sure that it was not in vain.

The seeds of totalitarian regimes are nurtured by misery and want. They spread and grow in the evil soil of poverty and strife. They reach their full growth when the hope of a people for a better life has died.

We must keep that hope alive.

The free peoples of the world look to us for support in maintaining their freedoms.

If we falter in our leadership, we may endanger the peace of the world—and we shall surely endanger the welfare of our own nation.

Great responsibilities have been placed upon us by the swift movement of events.

I am confident that the Congress will face these responsibilities squarely.

— 45 —

THE MARSHALL PLAN,
JUNE 5, 1947 [49]

By 1947 it became clear that the hoped-for economic recovery of Europe was not taking place. The United States now possessed 40 per cent of the world's income, and the rise of prices in the United States reduced the purchasing power of dollar loans to European governments. On June 5, 1947, Secretary of State George C. Marshall, in an address at Harvard University, laid down the principles that were shortly to be embodied in the European Recovery Program. The Marshall Plan was devised as a comprehensive program of economic stabilization advantageous both to receivers and the giver. It was of major importance in checking the spread of communism in Western Europe. Some four and a half billion dollars were spent in the first year of the plan (1948-1949) with the aim of making the various countries of the world self-supporting.

✓   ✓   ✓

I need not tell you, gentlemen, that the world situation is very serious. That must be apparent to all intelligent people. I think one difficulty is that the problem is one of such enormous complexity that the very mass of facts presented to the public by press and radio make it exceedingly difficult for the man in the street to reach a clear appraisement of the situation. Furthermore, the people of this country are distant from the troubled areas

[49] *The New York Times,* June 6, 1947.

of the earth and it is hard for them to comprehend the
plight and consequent reactions on their governments in
connection with our efforts to promote peace in the
world.

In considering the requirements for the rehabilitation
of Europe the physical loss of life, the visible destruction
of cities, factories, mines and railroads was correctly
estimated, but it has become obvious during recent months
that this visible destruction was probably less serious than
the dislocation of the entire fabric of European economy.
For the past ten years conditions have been highly abnormal.

The feverish preparation for war and the more feverish
maintenance of the war effort engulfed all aspects of national economies. Machinery has fallen into disrepair or
is entirely obsolete. Under the arbitrary and destructive
Nazi rule, virtually every possible enterprise was geared
into the German war machine. Long-standing commercial
ties, private institutions, banks, insurance companies and
shipping companies disappeared, through loss of capital,
absorption through nationalization or by simple destruction.

In many countries, confidence in the local currency has
been severely shaken. The breakdown of the business
structure of Europe during the war was complete. Recovery has been seriously retarded by the fact that two
years after the close of hostilities a peace agreement with
Germany and Austria has not been agreed upon. But
even given a more prompt solution of these difficult problems, the rehabilitation of the economic structure of Europe quite evidently will require a much longer time and
greater effort than had been foreseen.

There is a phase of this matter which is both interest-
ing and serious. The farmer has always produced the
foodstuffs to exchange with the city dweller for the other
necessities of life. The division of labor is the basis of
modern civilization. At the present time it is threatened
with breakdown. The town and city industries are not
producing adequate goods to exchange with the food-
producing farmer. Raw materials and fuel are in short
supply. Machinery is lacking or worn out.

The farmer or the peasant cannot find the goods for

sale which he desires to purchase. So the sale of his farm produce for money which he cannot use, seems to him an unprofitable transaction. He, therefore, has withdrawn many fields from crop cultivation and is using them for grazing. He feeds more grain to stock and finds for himself and his family an ample supply of food, however short he may be on clothing and the other ordinary gadgets of civilization. Meanwhile, people in the cities are short of food and fuel. So the governments are forced to use their foreign money and credits to procure these necessities abroad. This process exhausts funds which are urgently needed for reconstruction. Thus a very serious situation is rapidly developing which bodes no good for the world. The modern system of the division of labor upon which the exchange of products is based is in danger of breaking down.

The truth of the matter is that Europe's requirements for the next three or four years of foreign food and other essential products—principally from America—are so much greater than her present ability to pay that she must have substantial additional help, or face economic, social and political deterioration of a very grave character.

The remedy lies in breaking the vicious circle and restoring the confidence of the European people in the economic future of their own countries and of Europe as a whole. The manufacturer and the farmer throughout wide areas must be able and willing to exchange their products for currencies, the continuing value of which is not open to question.

Aside from the demoralizing effect on the world at large and the possibilities of disturbances arising as a result of the desperation of the people concerned, the consequences to the economy of the United States should be apparent to all. It is logical that the United States should do whatever it is able to do to assist in the return of normal economic health to the world, without which there can be no political stability and no assured peace.

Our policy is directed not against any country or doctrine but against hunger, poverty, desperation and chaos. Its purpose should be the revival of a working economy in the world so as to permit the emergence of political and social conditions in which free institutions can exist. Such assistance, I am convinced, must not be on a piece-meal basis as various crises develop. Any assistance that this government may develop in the future should provide a cure rather than a mere palliative.

Any government that is willing to assist in the task of recovery will find full cooperation, I am sure, on the part of the United States Government. Any government which maneuvers to block the recovery of other countries cannot expect help from us. Furthermore, governments, political parties or groups which seek to perpetuate human misery in order to profit therefrom politically or otherwise will encounter the opposition of the United States.

It is already evident that, before the United States Government can proceed much further in its efforts to alleviate the situation and help start the European world on its way to recovery, there must be some agreement among the countries of Europe as to the requirements of the situation and the part those countries themselves will take in order to give proper effect to whatever action might be undertaken by this Government. It would be neither fitting nor efficacious for this Government to undertake to draw up unilaterally a program designed to place Europe on its feet economically. This is the business of the Europeans. The initiative, I think, must come from Europe. The role of this country should consist of friendly aid in the drafting of a European program and of later support of such a program so far as it may be practical for us to do so. The program should be a joint one, agreed to by a number, if not all European nations.

An essential part of any successful action on the part of the United States is an understanding on the part of the people of America of the character of the problem and the remedies to be applied. Political passion and prejudice should have no part. With foresight, and a willingness on the part of our people to face up to the vast responsibility which history has clearly placed upon our country, the difficulties I have outlined can and will be overcome.

— 46 —

EXPULSION OF MARSHAL TITO AND YUGOSLAVIA FROM THE COMINFORM, JUNE, 1948 [50]

Marshal Tito, the Yugoslav Communist leader, refused to accept the rôle of Kremlin satellite and demanded the right to run his country in his own way. In June, 1948, Tito, his associates, and the Yugoslav Communist Party were officially expelled from the Cominform. This marked the first successful attempt of a potential satellite state to break away from Russian control.

✔   ✔   ✔

The Cominform finds that the leadership of the Yugoslav Communist Party creates a hateful policy in relation to the Soviet Union and to the All-Communist Union of Bolsheviks. The leading persons of the Communist Party of Yugoslavia take a standpoint unworthy of Communists . . . and they treat the Soviet Union in the same manner as they treat the bourgeois states. . . . The Cominform condemns these anti-Soviet conceptions of leading members of the Yugoslav Communist Party as incompatible with Marxism-Leninism and as suitable for nationalists. The leading members of the Yugoslav Communist Party are slipping off the Marx-Lenin path to the nationalist, kulak road.

[50] Quoted in Robert Ergang, *Europe in Our Time* (Boston, 1953), p. 820.

— 47 —

THE UNIVERSAL DECLARATION OF THE RIGHTS OF MAN, DECEMBER, 1948 [51]

The General Assembly of the United Nations in December, 1948, without a dissenting vote (48 voting, 8 abstaining) adopted a Universal Declaration of the Rights of Man, the first attempt in history to set down the minimum rights which every person should enjoy. The first ten of the thirty articles follow.

ARTICLE 1. All human beings are born free and equal in dignity and rights. They are endowed with reason and conscience and should act toward one another in a spirit of brotherhood.

ARTICLE 2. (1) Everyone is entitled to all rights and freedoms set forth in this declaration, without distinction of any kind, such as race, color, sex, language, religion, political or other opinion, national or social origin, property, birth or other status.

(2) Furthermore, no distinction shall be made on the basis of the political, jurisdictional or international status of the country or territory to which a person belongs, whether this territory be an independent, Trust, Non-Self-Governing territory, or under any other limitation of sovereignty.

[51] Courtesy of the United Nations.

ARTICLE 3. Everyone has the right to life, liberty and the security of the person.

ARTICLE 4. No one shall be held in slavery or servitude; slavery and the slave trade shall be prohibited in all their forms.

ARTICLE 5. No one shall be subjected to torture or to cruel inhuman or degrading treatment or punishment.

ARTICLE 6. Everyone has the right of recognition everywhere as a person before the law.

ARTICLE 7. All are equal before the law and are entitled without any discrimination to equal protection before the law. All are entitled to equal protection against any discrimination in violation of this Declaration and against any incitement to such discrimination.

ARTICLE 8. Everyone has the right to an effective remedy by the competent national tribunals for acts violating the fundamental rights granted to him by the constitution or by law.

ARTICLE 9. No one shall be subjected to arbitrary arrest, detention or exile.

ARTICLE 10. Everyone is entitled in full equality to a fair and public hearing by an independent and impartial tribunal in the determination of his rights and obligations and of any criminal charge against him.

— 48 —

THE NORTH ATLANTIC TREATY, APRIL 4, 1949[52]

The North Atlantic Treaty was drawn up in the fall of 1948 after the foreign ministers of Great Britain, France, Belgium, The Netherlands and Luxemburg had invited the United States and Canada to join in a security alliance for mutual defense. Signed by these nations and Norway, Denmark, Iceland, Italy, and Portugal, this treaty announced support of the United Nations, the desire to settle differences peacefully, and agreement to develop individual and collective capacities to resist attack. It was obviously designed to prevent further Russian expansion.

✦   ✦   ✦

PREAMBLE. The parties to this treaty reaffirm their faith in the purposes and principles of the Charter of the United Nations and their desire to live in peace with all peoples and all governments.

They are determined to safeguard the freedom, common heritage and civilization of their peoples, founded on the principles of democracy, individual liberty and the rule of law.

They seek to promote stability and well-being in the North Atlantic area.

They are resolved to unite their efforts for collective defense and for the preservation of peace and security.

[52] *The New York Times,* March 19, 1949. The text was published before the official signing.

They therefore agree to this North Atlantic Treaty:

ARTICLE 1. The parties undertake, as set forth in the Charter of the United Nations, to settle any international disputes in which they may be involved by peaceful means in such a manner that international peace and security, and justice, are not endangered, and to refrain in their international relations from the threat or use of force in any manner inconsistent with the purposes of the United Nations.

ARTICLE 2. The parties will contribute toward the further development of peaceful and friendly international relations by strengthening their free institutions, by bringing about a better understanding of the principles upon which these institutions are founded, and by promoting conditions of stability and well-being. They will seek to eliminate conflict in their international economic policies and will encourage economic collaboration between any or all of them.

ARTICLE 3. In order more effectively to achieve the objectives of this treaty, the parties, separately and jointly, by means of continuous and effective self-help and mutual aid, will maintain and develop their individual and collective capacity to resist armed attack.

ARTICLE 4. The parties will consult together whenever, in the opinion of any of them, the territorial integrity, political independence or security of any of the parties is threatened.

ARTICLE 5. The parties agree that an armed attack against one or more of them in Europe or North America shall be considered an attack against them all; and consequently they agree that, if such an armed attack occurs, each of them, in exercise of the right of individual or collective self-defense recognized by Article 51 of the Charter of the United Nations, will assist the party or parties so attacked by taking forthwith, individually and in concert with the other parties, such action as it deems necessary, including the use of armed force, to restore and maintain the security of the North Atlantic area.

Any such armed attack and all measures taken as a result thereof shall immediately be reported to the Security Council. Such measures shall be terminated when the Security Council has taken the measures necessary to restore and maintain international peace and security.

ARTICLE 6. For the purpose of Article 5 an armed attack on one or more of the parties is deemed to include an armed attack on the territory of any of the parties in Europe or North America, on the Algerian Departments of France, on the occupation forces of any party in Europe, on the islands under the jurisdiction of any party in the North Atlantic area north of the Tropic of Cancer or on the vessels or aircraft in this area of any of the parties.

ARTICLE 7. This treaty does not affect, and shall not be interpreted as affecting, in any way the rights and obligations under the Charter of the parties which are members of the United Nations, or the primary responsibility of the Security Council for the maintenance of international peace and security.

ARTICLE 8. Each party declares that none of the international engagements now in force between it and any other of the parties or any third state is in conflict with the provisions of this treaty, and undertakes not to enter into any international engagement in conflict with this treaty.

ARTICLE 9. The parties hereby establish a Council, on which each of them shall be represented, to consider matters concerning the implementation of this treaty. The Council shall be so organized as to be able to meet promptly at any time. The Council shall set up such subsidiary bodies as may be necessary; in particular it shall establish immediately a defense committee which shall recommend measures for the implementation of Articles 3 and 5.

ARTICLE 10. The parties may, by unanimous agreement, invite any other European state in a position to further the principles of this treaty and to contribute to the security of the North Atlantic area to accede to this treaty. Any state so invited may become a party to the treaty by depositing its instrument of accession with the Government of the United States of America. The Government of the United States of America will inform each of the parties of the deposit of each such instrument of accession.

ARTICLE 11. This treaty shall be ratified and its provisions carried out by the parties in accordance with their respective constitutional processes. The instruments of ratification shall be deposited as soon as possible with the Government of the United States of America, which will notify all the other signatories of each deposit. The treaty shall enter into force between the states which have ratified it as soon as the ratifications of the majority of the signatories, including the ratifications of Belgium, Canada, France, Luxembourg, the Netherlands, the United Kingdom and the United States, have been deposited and shall come into effect with respect to other states on the date of the deposit of their ratifications.

ARTICLE 12. After the treaty has been in force for ten years, or at any time thereafter, the parties shall, if any of them so requests, consult together for the purpose of reviewing the treaty, having regard for the factors then affecting peace and security in the North Atlantic area, including the development of universal as well as regional arrangements under the Charter of the United Nations for the maintenance of international peace and security.

ARTICLE 13. After the treaty has been in force for twenty years, any party may cease to be a party one year after its notice of denunciation has been given to the Government of the United States of America, which will inform the Governments of the other parties of the deposit of each notice of denunciation.

ARTICLE 14. This treaty, of which the English and French texts are equally authentic, shall be deposited in the archives of the Government of the United States of America. Duly certified copies thereof will be transmitted by that Government to the Governments of the other signatories.

IN WITNESS WHEREOF, the undersigned plenipotentiaries have signed this treaty.

— 49 —

FINAL ACT OF NINE-POWER CONFERENCE ON ARMING WEST GERMANY, LONDON, SEPTEMBER 27–OCTOBER 3, 1954 [53]

On October 3, 1954, nine Western powers signed an agreement in London to integrate West Germany politically and militarily in Western Europe. The French National Assembly, which on August 30, 1954, had refused to ratify the European Defense Agreement for a supranational West European set-up, on October 12 approved in principle the London agreements. Following are the introductory sections to the Final Act of London.

✦   ✦   ✦

The conference of the nine powers, Belgium, Canada, France, German Federal Republic, Italy, Luxembourg, Netherlands, United Kingdom of Great Britain and Northern Ireland and United States, met in London from Tuesday, Sept. 28 to Sunday, Oct. 3. It dealt with the most important issues facing the Western world, security and European integration within the framework of a developing Atlantic community dedicated to peace and freedom. In this connection the conference considered how to assure the full association of the German Federal

---

[53] *The New York Times,* October 4, 1954.

Republic with the West and the German defense contribution.

Belgium was represented by His Excellency M. P. H. Spaak.

Canada was represented by the Hon. L. B. Pearson.

France was represented by His Excellency M. P. Mendés-France.

The Federal Republic of Germany was represented by His Excellency Dr. K. Adenauer.

Italy was represented by His Excellency Prof. G. Martino.

Luxembourg was represented by His Excellency M. J. Bech.

The Netherlands was represented by His Excellency J. W. Beyen.

The United Kingdom of Great Britain and Northern Ireland was represented by Right Hon. A. Eden, M. C., M. P.

The United States of America was represented by the Hon. J. F. Dulles.

All the decisions of the conference formed part of one general settlement which is, directly or indirectly, of concern to all the NATO powers and which will therefore be submitted to the North Atlantic Council for information or decision.

I

GERMANY

The Governments of France, the United Kingdom and the United States declare that their policy is to end the occupation regime in the Federal Republic as soon as possible, to revoke the Occupation Statute and to abolish the Allied High Commission. The three Governments will continue to discharge certain responsibilities in Germany arising out of the international situation.

It is intended to conclude, and to bring into force as soon as the necessary parliamentary procedures have been completed, the appropriate instruments for these purposes. General agreement has already been reached on the content of these instruments and representatives of the four governments will meet in the very near future to complete the final texts. The agreed arrangements may be put into effect either before or simultaneously with the arrangements for the German defense contribution.

As these arrangements will take a little time to complete, the three governments have in the meantime issued the following declaration of intent:

"Recognizing that a great country can no longer be deprived of the rights properly belonging to a free and democratic people, and

"Desiring to associate the Federal Republic of Germany on a footing of equality with their efforts for peace and security.

"The governments of France, the United Kingdom, the United States of America desire to end the occupation regime as soon as possible.

"The fulfillment of this policy calls for the settlement of problems of detail in order to liquidate the past and to prepare for the future, and requires the completion of appropriate parliamentary procedures.

"In the meantime, the three governments are instructing their High Commissioners to act forthwith in accordance with the spirit of the above policy. In particular, the High Commissioners will not use the powers which are to be relinquished, unless in agreement with the Federal Government, except in the fields of disarmament and demilitarization and in cases where the Federal Government has not been able for legal reasons to take the action or assume the obligations contemplated in the agreed arrangement." . . .

— 50 —

CHARTER OF THE UNITED
NATIONS[54]

Twentieth-century man has become increasingly aware that world government is a necessary corrective to the dangers of aggressive nationalism, and that only coöperative international control can save man from his own destructive genius. The Charter of the United Nations, signed on June 26, 1945, is of such importance for the future of mankind that it is reproduced *in toto* here.

✓   ✓   ✓

*WE THE PEOPLES
OF THE UNITED NATIONS
DETERMINED*

to save succeeding generations from the scourge of war, which twice in our lifetime has brought untold sorrow to mankind, and

to reaffirm faith in fundamental human rights, in the dignity and worth of the human person, in the equal rights of men and women and of nations large and small, and

to establish conditions under which justice and respect for the obligations arising from treaties and other sources of international law can be maintained, and

to promote social progress and better standards of life in larger freedom,

[54] By permission of The United Nations.

AND FOR THESE ENDS

to practice tolerance and live together in peace with one another as good neighbors, and

to unite our strength to maintain international peace and security, and

to ensure, by the acceptance of principles and the institution of methods, that armed force shall not be used, save in the common interest, and

to employ international machinery for the promotion of the economic and social advancement of all peoples,

HAVE RESOLVED TO
COMBINE OUR EFFORTS TO
ACCOMPLISH THESE AIMS.

Accordingly, our respective Governments, through representatives assembled in the city of San Francisco, who have exhibited their full powers found to be in good and due form, have agreed to the present Charter of the United Nations and do hereby establish an international organization to be known as the United Nations.

Chapter I
PURPOSES AND PRINCIPLES

Article 1

The Purposes of the United Nations are:

1. To maintain international peace and security, and to that end: to take effective collective measures for the prevention and removal of threats to the peace, and for the suppression of acts of aggression or other breaches of the peace, and to bring about by peaceful means, and in conformity with the principles of justice and international law, adjustment or settlement of internationl disputes or situations which might lead to a breach of the peace;

2. To develop friendly relations among nations based on respect for the principle of equal rights and self-determination of peoples, and to take other appropriate measures to strengthen universal peace;

3. To achieve international cooperation in solving international problems of an economic, social, cultural, or humanitarian character, and in promoting and encouraging respect for human rights and for fundamental freedoms for all without distinction as to race, sex, language, or religion; and

4. To be a center for harmonizing the actions of nations in the attainment of these common ends.

Article 2

The Organization and its Members, in pursuit of the Purposes stated in Article 1, shall act in accordance with the following Principles.

1. The Organization is based on the principle of the sovereign equality of all its Members.

2. All Members, in order to ensure to all of them the rights and benefits resulting from membership, shall fulfil in good faith the obligations assumed by them in accordance with the present Charter.

3. All Members shall settle their international disputes by peaceful means in such a manner that international peace and security, and justice, are not endangered.

4. All Members shall refrain in their international relations from the threat or use of force against the territorial integrity or political independence of any state, or in any other manner inconsistent with the Purposes of the United Nations.

5. All Members shall give the United Nations every assistance in any action it takes in accordance with the present Charter, and shall refrain from giving assistance to any state against which the United Nations is taking preventive or enforcement action.

6. The Organization shall ensure that states which are not Members of the United Nations act in accordance with these Principles so far as may be necessary for the maintenance of international peace and security.

7. Nothing contained in the present Charter shall authorize the United Nations to intervene in matters which are essentially within the domestic jurisdiction of any state or shall require the Members to submit such matters to settlement under the present Charter; but this

principle shall not prejudice the application of enforcement measures under Chapter VII.

CHAPTER II
MEMBERSHIP

Article 3

The original Members of the United Nations shall be the states which, having participated in the United Nations Conference on International Organization at San Francisco, or having previously signed the Declaration by United Nations of January 1, 1942, sign the present Charter and ratify it in accordance with Article 110.

Article 4

1. Membership in the United Nations is open to all other peace-loving states which accept the obligations contained in the present Charter and, in the judgment of the Organization, are able and willing to carry out these obligations.

2. The admission of any such state to membership in the United Nations will be effected by a decision of the General Assembly upon the recommendation of the Security Council.

Article 5

A Member of the United Nations against which preventive or enforcement action has been taken by the Security Council may be suspended from the exercise of the rights and privileges of membership by the General Assembly upon the recommendation of the Security Council. The exercise of these rights and privileges may be restored by the Security Council.

Article 6

A Member of the United Nations which has persistently violated the Principles contained in the present Charter may be expelled from the Organization by the General Assembly upon the recommendation of the Security Council.

CHAPTER III
ORGANS

Article 7

1. There are established as the principal organs of the United Nations: a General Assembly, a Security Council, an Economic and Social Council, a Trusteeship Council, an International Court of Justice, and a Secretariat.

2. Such subsidiary organs as may be found necessary may be established in accordance with the present Charter.

Article 8

The United Nations shall place no restrictions on the eligibility of men and women to participate in any capacity and under conditions of equality in its principal and subsidiary organs.

CHAPTER IV
THE GENERAL ASSEMBLY

Composition

Article 9

1. The General Assembly shall consist of all the Members of the United Nations.

2. Each Member shall have not more than five representatives in the General Assembly.

Functions and Powers

Article 10

The General Assembly may discuss any questions or any matters within the scope of the present Charter or relating to the powers and functions of any organs provided for in the present Charter, and, except as provided in Article 12, may make recommendations to the Members of the United Nations or to the Security Council or to both on any such questions or matters.

Article 11

1. The General Assembly may consider the general principles of cooperation in the maintenance of inter-

national peace and security, including the principles governing disarmament and the regulation of armaments, and may make recommendations with regard to such principles to the Members or to the Security Council or to both.

2. The General Assembly may discuss any questions relating to the maintenance of international peace and security brought before it by any Member of the United Nations, or by the Security Council, or by a state which is not a Member of the United Nations in accordance with Article 35, paragraph 2, and, except as provided in Article 12, may make recommendations with regard to any such question to the state or states concerned or to the Security Council or to both. Any such question on which action is necessary shall be referred to the Security Council by the General Assembly either before or after discussion.

3. The General Assembly may call the attention of the Security Council to situations which are likely to endanger international peace and security.

4. The powers of the General Assembly set forth in this Article shall not limit the general scope of Article 10.

Article 12

1. While the Security Council is exercising in respect of any dispute or situation the functions assigned to it in the present Charter, the General Assembly shall not make any recommendations with regard to that dispute or situation unless the Security Council so requests.

2. The Secretary-General, with the consent of the Security Council, shall notify the General Assembly at each session of any matters relative to the maintenance of international peace and security which are being dealt with by the Security Council and shall similarly notify the General Assembly, or the Members of the United Nations if the General Assembly is not in session, immediately the Security Council ceases to deal with such matters.

Article 13

1. The General Assembly shall initiate studies and make recommendations for the purpose of:
  a. promoting international cooperation in the political

field and encouraging the progressive development of international law and its codification;

b. promoting international cooperation in the economic, social, cultural, educational, and health fields, and assisting in the realization of human rights and fundamental freedoms for all without distinction as to race, sex, language, or religion.

2. The further responsibilities, functions and powers of the General Assembly with respect to matters mentioned in paragraph 1 (b) above are set forth in Chapters IX and X.

Article 14

Subject to the provisions of Article 12, the General Assembly may recommend measures for the peaceful adjustment of any situation, regardless of origin, which it deems likely to impair the general welfare or friendly relations among nations, including situations resulting from a violation of the provisions of the present Charter setting forth the Purposes and Principles of the United Nations.

Article 15

1. The General Assembly shall receive and consider annual and special reports from the Security Council; these reports shall include an account of the measures that the Security Council has decided upon or taken to maintain international peace and security.

2. The General Assembly shall receive and consider reports from the other organs of the United Nations.

Article 16

The General Assembly shall perform such functions with respect to the international trusteeship system as are assigned to it under Chapters XII and XIII, including the approval of trusteeship agreements for areas not designated as strategic.

Article 17

1. The General Assembly shall consider and approve the budget of the Organization.

2. The expenses of the Organization shall be borne by the Members as apportioned by the General Assembly.

3. The General Assembly shall consider and approve any financial and budgetary arrangements with specialized agencies referred to in Article 57 and shall examine the administrative budgets of such specialized agencies with a view to making recommendations to the agencies concerned.

Voting

Article 18

1. Each member of the General Assembly shall have one vote.

2. Decisions of the General Assembly on important questions shall be made by a two-thirds majority of the members present and voting. These questions shall include: recommendations with respect to the maintenance of international peace and security, the election of the non-permanent members of the Security Council, the election of the members of the Economic and Social Council, the election of members of the Trusteeship Council in accordance with paragraph 1(c) of Article 86, the admission of new Members to the United Nations, the suspension of the rights and privileges of membership, the expulsion of Members, questions relating to the operation of the trusteeship system, and budgetary questions.

3. Decisions on other questions, including the determination of additional categories of questions to be decided by a two-thirds majority, shall be made by a majority of the members present and voting.

Article 19

A Member of the United Nations which is in arrears in the payment of its financial contributions to the Organization shall have no vote in the General Assembly if the amount of its arrears equals or exceeds the amount of the contributions due from it for the preceding two full years. The General Assembly may, nevertheless, permit such a Member to vote if it is satisfied that the failure to pay is due to conditions beyond the control of the Member.

Procedure

Article 20

The General Assembly shall meet in regular annual sessions and in such special sessions as occasion may require. Special sessions shall be convoked by the Secretary-General at the request of the Security Council or of a majority of the Members of the United Nations.

Article 21

The General Assembly shall adopt its own rules of procedure. It shall elect its President for each session.

Article 22

The General Assembly may establish such subsidiary organs as it deems necessary for the performance of its functions.

CHAPTER V
THE SECURITY COUNCIL

Composition

Article 23

1. The Security Council shall consist of eleven Members of the United Nations. The Republic of China, France, the Union of Soviet Socialist Republics, the United Kingdom of Great Britain and Northern Ireland, and the United States of America shall be permanent members of the Security Council. The General Assembly shall elect six other Members of the United Nations to be non-permanent members of the Security Council, due regard being specially paid, in the first instance to the contribution of Members of the United Nations to the maintenance of international peace and security and to the other purposes of the Organization, and also to equitable geographical distribution.

2. The non-permanent members of the Security Council shall be elected for a term of two years. In the first election of the non-permanent members, however, three shall be chosen for a term of one year. A retiring member shall not be eligible for immediate re-election.

3. Each member of the Security Council shall have one representative.

Functions and Powers

Article 24

1. In order to ensure prompt and effective action by the United Nations, its Members confer on the Security Council primary responsibility for the maintenance of international peace and security, and agree that in carrying out its duties under this responsibility the Security Council acts on their behalf.

2. In discharging these duties the Security Council shall act in accordance with the Purposes and Principles of the United Nations. The specific powers granted to the Security Council for the discharge of these duties are laid down in Chapters VI, VII, VIII, and XII.

3. The Security Council shall submit annual and, when necessary, special reports to the General Assembly for its consideration.

Article 25

The Members of the United Nations agree to accept and carry out the decisions of the Security Council in accordance with the present Charter.

Article 26

In order to promote the establishment and maintenance of international peace and security with the least diversion for armaments of the world's human and economic resources, the Security Council shall be responsible for formulating, with the assistance of the Military Staff Committee referred to in Article 47, plans to be submitted to the Members of the United Nations for the establishment of a system for the regulation of armaments.

Voting

Article 27

1. Each member of the Security Council shall have one vote.

2. Decisions of the Security Council on procedural

matters shall be made by an affirmative vote of seven members.

3. Decisions of the Security Council on all other matters shall be made by an affirmative vote of seven members including the concurring votes of the permanent members; provided that, in decisions under Chapter VI, and under paragraph 3 of Article 52, a party to dispute shall abstain from voting.

Procedure

Article 28

1. The Security Council shall be so organized as to be able to function continuously. Each member of the Security Council shall for this purpose be represented at all times at the seat of the Organization.

2. The Security Council shall hold periodic meetings at which each of its members may, if it so desires, be represented by a member of the government or by some other specially designated representative.

3. The Security Council may hold meetings at such places other than the seat of the Organization as in its judgment will best facilitate its work.

Article 29

The Security Council may establish such subsidiary organs as it deems necessary for the performance of its functions.

Article 30

The Security Council shall adopt its own rules of procedure, including the method of selecting its President.

Article 31

Any Member of the United Nations which is not a member of the Security Council may participate, without vote, in the discussion of any question brought before the Security Council whenever the latter considers that the interests of that Member are specially affected.

Article 32

Any Member of the United Nations which is not a member of the Security Council or any state which is not a Member of the United Nations, if it is a party to a dispute under consideration by the Security Council, shall be invited to participate, without vote, in the discussion relating to the dispute. The Security Council shall lay down such conditions as it deems just for the participation of a state which is not a Member of the United Nations.

CHAPTER VI
PACIFIC SETTLEMENT OF DISPUTES

Article 33

1. The parties to any dispute, the continuance of which is likely to endanger the maintenance of international peace and security, shall, first of all, seek a solution by negotiation, enquiry, mediation, conciliation, arbitration, judicial settlement, resort to regional agencies or arrangements, or other peaceful means of their own choice.

2. The Security Council shall, when it deems necessary, call upon the parties to settle their dispute by such means.

Article 34

The Security Council may investigate any dispute, or any situation which might lead to international friction or give rise to a dispute, in order to determine whether the continuance of the dispute or situation is likely to endanger the maintenance of international peace and security.

Article 35

1. Any Member of the United Nations may bring any dispute, or any situation of the nature referred to in Article 34, to the attention of the Security Council or of the General Assembly.

2. A state which is not a Member of the United Nations may bring to the attention of the Security Council or of the General Assembly any dispute to which it is a party if it accepts in advance, for the purposes of the dispute, the obligations of pacific settlement provided in the present Charter.

3. The proceedings of the General Assembly in respect

to matters brought to its attention under this Article will be subject to the provisions of Articles 11 and 12.

Article 36

1. The Security Council may, at any stage of a dispute of the nature referred to in Article 33 or of a situation of like nature, recommend appropriate procedures or methods of adjustment.

2. The Security Council should take into consideration any procedures for the settlement of the dispute which have already been adopted by the parties.

3. In making recommendations under this Article the Security Council should also take into consideration that legal disputes should as a general rule be referred by the parties to the International Court of Justice in accordance with the provisions of the Statute of the Court.

Article 37

1. Should the parties to a dispute of the nature referred to in Article 33 fail to settle it by the means indicated in that Article, they shall refer it to the Security Council.

2. If the Security Council deems that the continuance of the dispute is in fact likely to endanger the maintenance of international peace and security, it shall decide whether to take action under Article 36 or to recommend such terms of settlement as it may consider appropriate.

Article 38

Without prejudice to the provisions of Articles 33 to 37, the Security Council may, if all the parties to any dispute so request, make recommendations to the parties with a view to a pacific settlement of the dispute.

CHAPTER VII

ACTION WITH RESPECT TO THREATS TO THE PEACE, BREACHES OF THE PEACE, AND ACTS OF AGGRESSION

Article 39

The Security Council shall determine the existence of any threat to the peace, breach of the peace, or act of aggression and shall make recommendations, or decide what measures shall be taken in accordance with Articles 41 and 42, to maintain or restore international peace and security.

Article 40

In order to prevent an aggravation of the situation, the Security Council may, before making the recommendations or deciding upon the measures provided for in Article 39, call upon the parties concerned to comply with such provisional measures as it deems necessary or desirable. Such provisional measures shall be without prejudice to the rights, claims, or position of the parties concerned. The Security Council shall duly take account of failure to comply with such provisional measures.

Article 41

The Security Council may decide what measures not involving the use of armed force are to be employed to give effect to its decisions, and it may call upon the Members of the United Nations to apply such measures. These may include complete or partial interruption of economic relations and of rail, sea, air, postal, telegraphic, radio, and other means of communication, and the severance of diplomatic relations.

Article 42

Should the Security Council consider that measures provided for in Article 41 would be inadequate or have proved to be inadequate, it may take such action by air, sea, or land forces as may be necessary to maintain or restore international peace and security. Such action may include demonstrations, blockade, and other operations by air, sea, or land forces of Members of the United Nations.

Article 43

1. All Members of the United Nations, in order to contribute to the maintenance of international peace and security, undertake to make available to the Security Council, on its call and in accordance with a special agreement or agreements, armed forces, assistance, and

facilities, including rights of passage, necessary for the purpose of maintaining international peace and security.

2. Such agreement or agreements shall govern the numbers and types of forces, their degree of readiness and general location, and the nature of the facilities and assistance to be provided.

3. The agreement or agreements shall be negotiated as soon as possible on the initiative of the Security Council. They shall be concluded between the Security Council and Members or between the Security Council and groups of Members and shall be subject to ratification by the signatory states in accordance with their respective constitutional processes.

Article 44

When the Security Council has decided to use force it shall, before calling upon a Member not represented on it to provide armed forces in fulfillment of the obligations assumed under Article 43, invite that Member, if the Member so desires, to participate in the decisions of the Security Council concerning the employment of contingents of that Member's armed forces.

Article 45

In order to enable the United Nations to take urgent military measures, Members shall hold immediately available national air-force contingents for combined international enforcement action. The strength and degree of readiness of these contingents and plans for their combined action shall be determined, within the limits laid down in the special agreement or agreements referred to in Article 43, by the Security Council with the assistance of the Military Staff Committee.

Article 46

Plans for the application of armed force shall be made by the Security Council with the assistance of the Military Staff Committee.

Article 47

1. There shall be established a Military Staff Committee to advise and assist the Security Council on all

questions relating to the Security Council's military requirements for the maintenance of international peace and security, the employment and command of forces placed at its disposal, the regulation of armaments, and possible disarmament.

2. The Military Staff Committee shall consist of the Chiefs of Staff of the permanent members of the Security Council or their representatives. Any Member of the United Nations not permanently represented on the Committee shall be invited by the Committee to be associated with it when the efficient discharge of the Committee's responsibilities requires the participation of that Member in its work.

3. The Military Staff Committee shall be responsible under the Security Council for the strategic direction of any armed forces placed at the disposal of the Security Council. Questions relating to the command of such forces shall be worked out subsequently.

4. The Military Staff Committee, with the authorization of the Security Council and after consultation with appropriate regional agencies, may establish regional subcommittees.

Article 48

1. The action required to carry out the decisions of the Security Council for the maintenance of international peace and security shall be taken by all the Members of the United Nations or by some of them, as the Security Council may determine.

2. Such decisions shall be carried out by the Members of the United Nations directly and through their action in the appropriate international agencies of which they are members.

Article 49

The Members of the United Nations shall join in affording mutual assistance in carrying out the measures decided upon by the Security Council.

Article 50

If preventive or enforcement measures against any state are taken by the Security Council, any other state, whether a Member of the United Nations or not, which finds itself confronted with special economic problems arising from the carrying out of those measures shall have the right to consult the Security Council with regard to a solution of those problems.

Article 51

Nothing in the present Charter shall impair the inherent right of individual or collective self-defense if an armed attack occurs against a Member of the United Nations, until the Security Council has taken measures necessary to maintain international peace and security. Measures taken by Members in the exercise of this right of self-defense shall be immediately reported to the Security Council and shall not in any way affect the authority and responsibility of the Security Council under the present Charter to take at any time such action as it deems necessary in order to maintain or restore international peace and security.

CHAPTER VIII
REGIONAL ARRANGEMENTS

Article 52

1. Nothing in the present Charter precludes the existence of regional arrangements or agencies for dealing with such matters relating to the maintenance of international peace and security as are appropriate for regional action, provided that such arrangements or agencies and their activities are consistent with the Purposes and Principles of the United Nations.

2. The Members of the United Nations entering into such arrangements or constituting such agencies shall make every effort to achieve pacific settlement of local disputes through such regional arrangements or by such regional agencies before referring them to the Security Council.

3. The Security Council shall encourage the development of pacific settlement of local disputes through such regional arrangements or by such regional agencies either on the initiative of the states concerned or by reference from the Security Council.

4. This Article in no way impairs the application of Articles 34 and 35.

Article 53

1. The Security Council shall, where appropriate, utilize such regional arrangements or agencies for enforcement action under its authority. But no enforcement action shall be taken under regional arrangements or by regional agencies without the authorization of the Security Council, with the exception of measures against any enemy state, as defined in paragraph 2 of this Article, provided for pursuant to Article 107 or in regional arrangements directed against renewal of aggressive policy on the part of any such state, until such time as the Organization may, on request of the Governments concerned, be charged with the responsibility for preventing further aggression by such a state.

2. The term enemy state as used in paragraph 1 of this Article applies to any state which during the Second World War has been an enemy of any signatory of the present Charter.

Article 54

The Security Council shall at all times be kept fully informed of activities undertaken or in contemplation under regional arrangements or by regional agencies for the maintenance of international peace and security.

Chapter IX
INTERNATIONAL ECONOMIC AND SOCIAL COOPERATION

Article 55

With a view to the creation of conditions of stability and well-being which are necessary for peaceful and friendly relations among nations based on respect for the principle of equal rights and self-determination of peoples, the United Nations shall promote:

a. higher standards of living, full employment, and conditions of economic and social progress and development;

b. solutions of international economic, social, health,

and related problems; and international cultural and educational cooperation; and

c. universal respect for, and observance of, human rights and fundamental freedoms for all without distinction as to race, sex, language, or religion.

Article 56

All Members pledge themselves to take joint and separate action in cooperation with the Organization for the achievement of the purposes set forth in Article 55.

Article 57

1. The various specialized agencies, established by intergovernmental agreement and having wide international responsibilities, as defined in their basic instruments, in economic, social, cultural, educational, health, and related fields, shall be brought into relationship with the United Nations in accordance with the provisions of Article 63.

2. Such agencies thus brought into relationship with the United Nations are hereinafter referred to as specialized agencies.

Article 58

The Organization shall make recommendations for the coordination of the policies and activities of the specialized agencies.

Article 59

The Organization shall, where appropriate, initiate negotiations among the states concerned for the creation of any new specialized agencies required for the accomplishment of the purposes set forth in Article 55.

Article 60

Responsibility for the discharge of the functions of the Organization set forth in this Chapter shall be vested in the General Assembly and, under the authority of the General Assembly, in the Economic and Social Council, which shall have for this purpose the powers set forth in Chapter X.

Chapter X
THE ECONOMIC AND SOCIAL COUNCIL

Composition

Article 61

1. The Economic and Social Council shall consist of eighteen Members of the United Nations elected by the General Assembly.

2. Subject to the provisions of paragraph 3, six members of the Economic and Social Council shall be elected each year for a term of three years. A retiring member shall be eligible for immediate re-election.

3. At the first election, eighteen members of the Economic and Social Council shall be chosen. The term of office of six members so chosen shall expire at the end of one year, and of six other members at the end of two years, in accordance with arrangements made by the General Assembly.

4. Each member of the Economic and Social Council shall have one representative.

Functions and Powers

Article 62

1. The Economic and Social Council may make or initiate studies and reports with respect to international economic, social, cultural, educational, health, and related matters and may make recommendations with respect to any such matters to the General Assembly, to the Members of the United Nations, and to the specialized agencies concerned.

2. It may make recommendations for the purpose of promoting respect for, and observance of, human rights and fundamental freedoms for all.

3. It may prepare draft conventions for submission to the General Assembly, with respect to matters falling within its competence.

4. It may call, in accordance with the rules prescribed by the United Nations, international conferences on matters falling within its competence.

Article 63

1. The Economic and Social Council may enter into agreements with any of the agencies referred to in Article 57, defining the terms on which the agency concerned shall be brought into relationship with the United Nations. Such agreements shall be subject to approval by the General Assembly.

2. It may coordinate the activities of the specialized agencies through consultation with and recommendations to such agencies and through recommendations to the General Assembly and to the Members of the United Nations.

Article 64

1. The Economic and Social Council may take appropriate steps to obtain regular reports from the specialized agencies. It may make arrangements with the Members of the United Nations and with the specialized agencies to obtain reports on the steps taken to give effect to its own recommendations and to recommendations on matters falling within its competence made by the General Assembly.

2. It may communicate its observations on these reports to the General Assembly.

Article 65

The Economic and Social Council may furnish information to the Security Council and shall assist the Security Council upon its request.

Article 66

1. The Economic and Social Council shall perform such functions as fall within its competence in connection with the carrying out of the recommendations of the General Assembly.

2. It may, with the approval of the General Assembly, perform services at the request of Members of the United Nations and at the request of specialized agencies.

3. It shall perform such other functions as are specified elsewhere in the present Charter or as may be assigned to it by the General Assembly.

Voting

Article 67

1. Each member of the Economic and Social Council shall have one vote.
2. Decisions of the Economic and Social Council shall be made by a majority of the members present and voting.

Procedure

Article 68

The Economic and Social Council shall set up commissions in economic and social fields and for the promotion of human rights, and such other commissions as may be required for the performance of its functions.

Article 69

The Economic and Social Council shall invite any Member of the United Nations to participate, without vote, in its deliberations on any matter of particular concern to that Member.

Article 70

The Economic and Social Council may make arrangements for representatives of the specialized agencies to participate, without vote, in its deliberations and in those of the commissions established by it, and for its representatives to participate in the deliberations of the specialized agencies.

Article 71

The Economic and Social Council may make suitable arrangements for consultation with non-governmental organizations which are concerned with matters within its competence. Such arrangements may be made with international organizations and, where appropriate, with national organizations after consultation with the Member of the United Nations concerned.

Article 72

1. The Economic and Social Council shall adopt its own rules of procedure, including the method of selecting its President.

2. The Economic and Social Council shall meet as required in accordance with its rules, which shall include provision for the convening of meetings on the request of a majority of its members.

CHAPTER XI
DECLARATION REGARDING
NON-SELF-GOVERNING TERRITORIES

Article 73

Members of the United Nations which have or assume responsibilities for the administration of territories whose peoples have not yet attained a full measure of self-government recognize the principle that the interests of the inhabitants of these territories are paramount, and accept as a sacred trust the obligation to promote to the utmost, within the system of international peace and security established by the present Charter, the well-being of the inhabitants of these territories, and, to this end:

a. to ensure, with due respect for the culture of the peoples concerned, their political, economic, social, and educational advancement, their just treatment, and their protection against abuses;

b. to develop self-government, to take due account of the political aspirations of the peoples, and to assist them in the progressive development of their free political institutions, according to the particular circumstances of each territory and its peoples and their varying stages of advancement;

c. to further international peace and security;

d. to promote constructive measures of development, to encourage research, and to cooperate with one another and, when and where appropriate, with specialized international bodies with a view to the practical achievement of the social, economic, and scientific purposes set forth in this Article; and

e. to transmit regularly to the Secretary-General for information purposes, subject to such limitation as security and constitutional considerations may require, statistical and other information of a technical nature relating to economic, social, and educational conditions in the territories for which they are respectively responsible other than those territories to which Chapters XII and XIII apply.

Article 74

Members of the United Nations also agree that their policy in respect of the territories to which this Chapter applies, no less than in respect of their metropolitan areas, must be based on the general principle of good-neighborliness, due account being taken of the interests and well-being of the rest of the world, in social, economic, and commercial matters.

Chapter XII
INTERNATIONAL TRUSTEESHIP SYSTEM

Article 75

The United Nations shall establish under its authority an international trusteeship system for the administration and supervision of such territories as may be placed thereunder by subsequent individual agreements. These territories are hereinafter referred to as trust territories.

Article 76

The basic objectives of the trusteeship system, in accordance with the Purposes of the United Nations laid down in Article 1 of the present Charter, shall be:

a. to further international peace and security;

b. to promote the political, economic, social, and educational advancement of the inhabitants of the trust territories, and their progressive development towards self-government or independence as may be appropriate to the particular circumstances of each territory and its peoples and the freely expressed wishes of the peoples concerned, and as may be provided by the terms of each trusteeship agreement;

c. to encourage respect for human rights and for fundamental freedoms for all without distinction as to race, sex, language, or religion, and to encourage recognition of the interdependence of the peoples of the world; and

d. to ensure equal treatment in social, economic, and commercial matters for all Members of the United Nations and their nationals, and also equal treatment for the latter in the administration of justice, without prejudice to the attainment of the foregoing objectives and subject to the provisions of Article 80.

Article 77

1. The trusteeship system shall apply to such territories in the following categories as may be placed thereunder by means of trusteeship agreements:

    a. territories now held under mandate;

    b. territories which may be detached from enemy states as a result of the Second World War; and

    c. territories voluntarily placed under the system by states responsible for their administration.

2. It will be a matter for subsequent agreement as to which territories in the foregoing categories will be brought under the trusteeship system and upon what terms.

Article 78

The trusteeship system shall not apply to territories which have become Members of the United Nations, relationship among which shall be based on respect for the principle of sovereign equality.

Article 79

The terms of trusteeship for each territory to be placed under the trusteeship system, including any alteration or amendment, shall be agreed upon by the states directly concerned, including the mandatory power in the case of territories held under mandate by a Member of the United Nations, and shall be approved as provided for in Articles 83 and 85.

Article 80

1. Except as may be agreed upon in individual trusteeship agreements, made under Articles 77, 79, and 81, placing each territory under the trusteeship system, and until such agreements have been concluded, nothing in this Chapter shall be construed in or of itself to alter in any manner the rights whatsoever of any states or any peoples or the terms of existing international instruments to

which Members of the United Nations may respectively be parties.

2. Paragraph 1 of this Article shall not be interpreted as giving grounds for delay or postponement of the negotiation and conclusion of agreements for placing mandated and other territories under the trusteeship system as provided for in Article 77.

Article 81

The trusteeship agreement shall in each case include the terms under which the trust territory will be administered and designate the authority which will exercise the administration of the trust territory. Such authority, hereinafter called the administering authority, may be one or more states or the Organization itself.

Article 82

There may be designated, in any trusteeship agreement, a strategic area or areas which may include part or all of the trust territory to which the agreement applies, without prejudice to any special agreement or agreements made under Article 43.

Article 83

1. All functions of the United Nations relating to strategic areas, including the approval of the terms of the trusteeship agreements and of their alteration or amendment, shall be exercised by the Security Council.

2. The basic objectives set forth in Article 76 shall be applicable to the people of each strategic area.

3. The Security Council shall, subject to the provisions of the trusteeship agreements and without prejudice to security considerations, avail itself of the assistance of the Trusteeship Council to perform those functions of the United Nations under the trusteeship system relating to political, economic, social, and educational matters in the strategic areas.

Article 84

It shall be the duty of the administering authority to ensure that the trust territory shall play its part in the maintenance of international peace and security. To this end the administering authority may make use of volunteer forces, facilities, and assistance from the trust territory in carrying out the obligations towards the Security Council undertaken in this regard by the administering authority, as well as for local defense and the maintenance of law and order within the trust territory.

Article 85

1. The functions of the United Nations with regard to trusteeship agreements for all areas not designated as strategic, including the approval of the terms of the trusteeship agreements and of their alteration or amendment, shall be exercised by the General Assembly.

2. The Trusteeship Council, operating under the authority of the General Assembly, shall assist the General Assembly in carrying out these functions.

Chapter XIII
THE TRUSTEESHIP COUNCIL

Composition

Article 86

1. The Trusteeship Council shall consist of the following Members of the United Nations:

    a. those Members administering trust territories;

    b. such of those Members mentioned by name in Article 23 as are not administering trust territories; and

    c. as many other Members elected for three-year terms by the General Assembly as may be necessary to ensure that the total number of members of the Trusteeship Council is equally divided between those Members of the United Nations which administer trust territories and those which do not.

2. Each member of the Trusteeship Council shall designate one specially qualified person to represent it therein.

Functions and Powers

Article 87

The General Assembly and, under its authority, the Trusteeship Council, in carrying out their functions, may:

a. consider reports submitted by the administering authority;

b. accept petitions and examine them in consultation with the administering authority;

c. provide for periodic visits to the respective trust territories at times agreed upon with the administering authority; and

d. take these and other actions in conformity with the terms of the trusteeship agreements.

Article 88

The Trusteeship Council shall formulate a questionnaire on the political, economic, social, and educational advancement of the inhabitants of each trust territory, and the administering authority for each trust territory within the competence of the General Assembly shall make an annual report to the General Assembly upon the basis of such questionnaire.

Voting

Article 89

1. Each member of the Trusteeship Council shall have one vote.

2. Decisions of the Trusteeship Council shall be made by a majority of the members present and voting.

Procedure

Article 90

1. The Trusteeship Council shall adopt its own rules of procedure, including the method of selecting its President.

2. The Trusteeship Council shall meet as required in accordance with its rules, which shall include provision for the convening of meetings on the request of a majority of its members.

Article 91

The Trusteeship Council shall, when appropriate, avail itself of the assistance of the Economic and Social Council and of the specialized agencies in regard to matters with which they are respectively concerned.

CHAPTER XIV
THE INTERNATIONAL COURT
OF JUSTICE

Article 92

The International Court of Justice shall be the principal judicial organ of the United Nations. It shall function in accordance with the annexed Statute, which is based upon the Statute of the Permanent Court of International Justice and forms an integral part of the present Charter.

Article 93

1. All Members of the United Nations are *ipso facto* parties to the Statute of the International Court of Justice.
2. A state which is not a Member of the United Nations may become a party to the Statute of the International Court of Justice on condition to be determined in each case by the General Assembly upon the recommendation of the Security Council.

Article 94

1. Each Member of the United Nations undertakes to comply with the decision of the International Court of Justice in any case to which it is a party.
2. If any party to a case fails to perform the obligations incumbent upon it under a judgment rendered by the Court, the other party may have recourse to the Security Council, which may, if it deems necessary, make recommendations or decide upon measures to be taken to give effect to the judgment.

Article 95

Nothing in the present Charter shall prevent Members of the United Nations from entrusting the solution of their differences to other tribunals by virtue of agreements already in existence or which may be concluded in the future.

Article 96

1. The General Assembly or the Security Council may request the International Court of Justice to give an advisory opinion on any legal question.

2. Other organs of the United Nations and specialized agencies, which may at any time be so authorized by the General Assembly, may also request advisory opinions of the Court on legal questions arising within the scope of their activities.

Chapter XV
THE SECRETARIAT

Article 97

The Secretariat shall comprise a Secretary-General and such staff as the Organization may require. The Secretary-General shall be appointed by the General Assembly upon the recommendation of the Security Council. He shall be the chief administrative officer of the Organization.

Article 98

The Secretary-General shall act in that capacity in all meetings of the General Assembly, of the Security Council, of the Economic and Social Council, and of the Trusteeship Council, and shall perform such other functions as are entrusted to him by these organs. The Secretary-General shall make an annual report to the General Assembly on the work of the Organization.

Article 99

The Secretary-General may bring to the attention of the Security Council any matter which in his opinion may threaten the maintenance of international peace and security.

Article 100

1. In the performance of their duties the Secretary-General and the staff shall not seek or receive instructions from any government or from any other authority external to the Organization. They shall refrain from any

action which might reflect on their position as international officials responsible only to the Organization.

2. Each Member of the United Nations undertakes to respect the exclusively international character of the responsibilities of the Secretary-General and the staff and not to seek to influence them in the discharge of their responsibilities.

Article 101

1. The staff shall be appointed by the Secretary-General under regulations established by the General Assembly.

2. Appropriate staffs shall be permanently assigned to the Economic and Social Council, the Trusteeship Council, and, as required, to other organs of the United Nations. These staffs shall form a part of the Secretariat.

3. The paramount consideration in the employment of the staff and in the determination of the conditions of service shall be the necessity of securing the highest standards of efficiency, competence, and integrity. Due regard shall be paid to the importance of recruiting the staff on as wide a geographical basis as possible.

CHAPTER XVI
MISCELLANEOUS PROVISIONS

Article 102

1. Every treaty and every international agreement entered into by any Member of the United Nations after the present Charter comes into force shall as soon as possible be registered with the Secretariat and published by it.

2. No party to any such treaty or international agreement which has not been registered in accordance with the provisions of paragraph 1 of this Article may invoke that treaty or agreement before any organ of the United Nations.

Article 103

In the event of a conflict between the obligations of the Members of the United Nations under the present Charter and their obligations under any other international agreement, their obligations under the present Charter shall prevail.

Article 104

The Organization shall enjoy in the territory of each of its Members such legal capacity as may be necessary for the exercise of its functions and the fulfillment of its purposes.

Article 105

1. The Organization shall enjoy in the territory of each of its Members such privileges and immunities as are necessary for the fulfillment of its purposes.

2. Representatives of the Members of the United Nations and officials of the Organization shall similarly enjoy such privileges and immunities as are necessary for the independent exercise of their functions in connection with the Organization.

3. The General Assembly may make recommendations with a view to determining the details of the application of paragraphs 1 and 2 of this Article or may propose conventions to the Members of the United Nations for this purpose.

Chapter XVII
TRANSITIONAL SECURITY ARRANGEMENTS

Article 106

Pending the coming into force of such special agreements referred to in Article 43 as in the opinion of the Security Council enable it to begin the exercise of its responsibilities under Article 42, the parties to the Four-Nation Declaration, signed at Moscow, October 30, 1943, and France, shall, in accordance with the provisions of paragraph 5 of that Declaration, consult with one another and as occasion requires with other Members of the United Nations with a view to such joint action on behalf of the Organization as may be necessary for the purpose of maintaining international peace and security.

Article 107

Nothing in the present Charter shall invalidate or preclude action, in relation to any state which during the Second World War has been an enemy of any signatory to the present Charter, taken or authorized as a result of that war by the Governments having responsibility for such action.

CHAPTER XVIII
AMENDMENTS

Article 108

Amendments to the present Charter shall come into force for all Members of the United Nations when they have been adopted by a vote of two-thirds of the members of the General Assembly and ratified in accordance with their respective constitutional processes by two-thirds of the Members of the United Nations, including all the permanent members of the Security Council.

Article 109

1. A General Conference of the Members of the United Nations for the purpose of reviewing the present Charter may be held at a date and place to be fixed by a two-thirds vote of the members of the General Assembly and by a vote of any seven members of the Security Council. Each Member of the United Nations shall have one vote in the conference.

2. Any alteration of the present Charter recommended by a two-thirds vote of the conference shall take effect when ratified in accordance with their respective constitutional processes by two-thirds of the Members of the United Nations including all the permanent members of the Security Council.

3. If such a conference has not been held before the tenth annual session of the General Assembly following the coming into force of the present Charter, the proposal to call such a conference shall be placed on the agenda of that session of the General Assembly, and the conference shall be held if so decided by a majority vote of the

members of the General Assembly and by a vote of any seven members of the Security Council.

Chapter XIX
RATIFICATION AND SIGNATURE

Article 110

1. The present Charter shall be ratified by the signatory states in accordance with their respective constitutional processes.

2. The ratifications shall be deposited with the Government of the United States of America, which shall notify all the signatory states of each deposit as well as the Secretary-General of the Organization when he has been appointed.

3. The present Charter shall come into force upon the deposit of ratifications by the Republic of China, France, the Union of Soviet Socialist Republics, the United Kingdom of Great Britain and Northern Ireland, and the United States of America, and by a majority of the other signatory states. A protocol of the ratifications deposited shall thereupon be drawn up by the Government of the United States of America which shall communicate copies thereof to all the signatory states.

4. The states signatory to the present Charter which ratify it after it has come into force will become original Members of the United Nations on the date of the deposit of their respective ratifications.

Article 111

The present Charter, of which the Chinese, French, Russian, English, and Spanish texts are equally authentic, shall remain deposited in the archives of the Government of the United States of America. Duly certified copies thereof shall be transmitted by that Government to the Governments of the other signatory states.

In faith whereof the representatives of the Governments of the United Nations have signed the present Charter.

Done at the city of San Francisco the twenty-sixth day of June, one thousand nine hundred and forty-five.

VAN NOSTRAND ANVIL BOOKS already published